For more than fifteen years, I have been fortunate to minister with Dr. Kenneth Ulmer and Dr. James O. Davis. Over this span of time, I have witnessed firsthand these leaders cast vision and mobilize people to help to fulfill the vision. I cannot think of two more credible leaders who are qualified to write *The Forgotten Baptism: The Leadership Path to Fulfilling Your Vision*. Read it today!

David Sobrepena
Word of Hope Church
Philippines

There are countless leaders who have possessed a powerful vision but do not know how to fulfill it. In Dr. Kenneth Ulmer's and Dr. James O. Davis' latest book, *The Forgotten Baptism*, they have provided the leadership essentials to mobilizing people to fulfill the vision in the leader's lifetime. If you wish to achieve great outcomes with God, then *The Forgotten Baptism* is a must for you and your organization.

Dr. Timothy Hill
General Overseer
Church of God

Receiving a God-sized vision and the ability to execute it is a must for ministry success. Dr. Kenneth Ulmer and Dr. James O. Davis in *The Forgotten Baptism*, have masterfully outlined the powerful steps to visionary execution and effectiveness. I highly recommend you to purchase this must-read for you and your team!

Dr. Glenn Burris
President
Foursquare Church

Dr. James O. Davis and Dr. Kenneth Ulmer and I have been colleagues for many years. In *The Forgotten Baptism* they teach us how to discover, develop and deploy our personal vision maximum impact. This is a must book for our generation!

Dr. Ben Lerner
Zero To A Million Institute
Orlando, Florida

Visionary leadership is a must for local, national and international impact. Dr. Kenneth Ulmer and Dr. James O. Davis, in the latest book, *The Forgotten Baptism: The Leadership Path to Fulfilling Your Vision*, have provided the systematic steps to profound impact in this generation. Whether you lead a small, medium or large organization, this powerful read is for you!

Dr. James Merritt
Cross Point Church
Atlanta, Georgia

Visionary leadership with a plan of follow-through and execution are a must in every generation. Dr. Kenneth Ulmer and Dr. James O. Davis in *The Forgotten Baptism: The Leadership Path to Fulfilling Your Vision* have combined the "receiving of the vision" and the "releasing of the vision" for the leader who truly wants to impact his organization and mobilizing them for great success. Read it today and reap tomorrow!

Dr. David Wells
General Superintendent
Pentecostal Assemblies of God

We live in era of time, where old maps will not work in new lands. Visionary leaders are God's change agents bringing the unseen and uncreated into the seen and tangible world. Throughout the annals of history, visionary leaders have led people into new lands, new concepts and new ideas. In *The Forgotten Baptism*, Dr. James O. Davis and Dr. Kenneth Ulmer have powerfully revealed the secrets to harnessing huge vision and mobilizing people to fulfill the vision. This is a critical read for all leaders who wish to go beyond influence to impact!

Rev. Peter Mortlock
City Impact Church
Aukland, New Zealand

In the landmark book, *The Forgotten Baptism: The Leadership Path to Fulfilling Your Vision*, Dr. Kenneth Ulmer and Dr. James O. Davis, have synergized their expertise together to empower the next generation of visionary leaders for local, national and global impact. I encourage every Christian leader to obtain their personal copy right away.

Dr. George Wood
Assemblies of God
General Superintendent

In order for dreams to become destinies and vision to become victories, the Christian leader must cultivate and administrate a personal and professional plan for success. Dr. James O. Davis and Dr. Kenneth Ulmer in their latest book entitled, *The Forgotten Baptism: The Leadership Path to Fulfilling Your Vision*, creatively articulate the success strategies required to turning God-given vision into maximum impact. I highly recommend this life-changing resource to you and your fellow leaders.

Rev. Leon Fontaine
Springs Church
Winnipeg, Canada

Small dreams never inflame the hearts of great people! Dr. Kenneth Ulmer and Dr. James O. Davis. In *The Forgotten Baptism: The Leadership Path to Fulfilling Your Vision* teach us how to cast vision and mobilize people regardless the size of the vision... I cannot think of two more credible leaders who are qualified to help us to birth, build and broaden our vision. Read it today!

Dr. Samuel Rodriguez
President
North American Hispanic Leaders Conference

Visionary leaders are able to see the path first and view the plan long before it becomes a reality. In this generation, we desperately need Spirit-enabled visionary leaders who cast compelling vision and mobilize people from all walks of life to bring cultural transformation in our generation. In *The Forgotten Baptism: The Leadership Path to Fulfilling Your Vision*, Dr. James O. Davis and Dr. Kenneth Ulmer, have combined their expertise into a watershed book, destined to help equip powerful leaders in our world. Be sure to get yourself and team copies today!

Dr. Gustavo Crocker
General Superintendent, The Church of the Nazarene

You should purchase your copy of *The Forgotten Baptism* as soon as possible. Dr. James O. Davis and Dr. Kenneth Ulmer have delivered the quintessentials to understanding the qualities of vision and undertaking God-sized vision in your church, ministry or organization. When you are baptized in your thoughts through this powerful book, your life will never be the same!

Dr. David Mohan
New Life Assembly
Chennai, India

Dr. James O. Davis and Dr. Kenneth Ulmer are two of the finest communicators of this generation. In *The Forgotten Baptism: The Leadership Path to Fulfillng Your Vision*, will inspire you to dream bigger than ever before, along with illustrating the path to pursue great success in your personal and professional life. It is a must for every game-changing agent!

Dr. Suliasi Kurulo
World Harvest Center
Suva, Fiji

You will never leave a lasting impact without learning how to enlarge yourself to contain the size of your vision, expand your base of leaders to shoulder the vision and to encircle yourself with close allies when obstacles come to stop the fulfillment of the vision. In Dr. James O. Davis' and Dr. Kenneth Ulmer's latest book, *The Forgotten Baptism* will become the "visionary statement" of our generation. When you read this dynamic book, your mind, motivation and ministry will be revolutionized for many years to come!

Dr. Ademola Ishola
General Secretary, Emeritus
Nigerian Baptist Convention
Nigeria

Without vision people perish along with their dreams and destinies. I am thrilled to recommend *The Forgotten Baptism* to this emerging generation of visionary leaders. I believe the next generation will dream bigger-than-life dreams. My friends and co-laborers Dr. Kenneth Ulmer and Dr. James

O. Davis have written a masterpiece, showcasing the eight proven steps to truly impacting and transforming any size organization.

Dr. Alex Mitala
Chairman Emeritus New Birth Fellowship, Uganda

God is the author of vision for He saw the world before it was created and saw the plan of divine destiny before He ever spoke it. Throughout the annals of world history, Spirit-empowered, visionary leaders have led the way in revealing God's plan to their respective generations. Dr. James O. Davis and Dr. Kenneth Ulmer in *The Forgotten Baptism: The Leadership Path to Fulfilling Your Vision* have brought a biblical-based approach to receiving a God-given vision and releasing it in this generation. Get it and give it today!

Dr. Ronnie Floyd
Senior Pastor Cross Church
President Emeritus, Southern Baptist Convention

Why do some leaders succeed with the fulfillment of their vision, while other leaders fail to fulfill their vision? Dr. Kenneth Ulmer and Dr. James O. Davis, in *The Forgotten Baptism* answer these critical questions for success and reveal the path to finishing their vision. *The Forgotten Baptism* serves as a life-changing roadmap from the beginning to the end of the visionary quest for maximum impact.

Dr. Doug Beacham
General Superintendent
International Pentecostal Holiness Church

Dr. James O. Davis and Dr. Kenneth Ulmer have formed a powerful niche with *The Forgotten Baptism: The Leadership Path to Fulfilling Your Vision*. They are known for casting vision and mobilizing leaders worldwide. Every twenty-first century visionary leader, who wants to create and complete their vision, must learn the lessons from this cataclysmic book!

Dr. Jo Anne Lyon
Wesleyans
General Superintendent, Emeritus

Dr. Kenneth Ulmer and Dr. James O. Davis are two of my closest friends in ministry today. We have ministered together throughout the world and have synergized our efforts together for the advancement of the Kingdom of God. I cannot think of two more qualified servants to write *The Forgotten Baptism: The Leadership Path to Fulfilling Your Vision* than them. Ken and James have continuously cast a compelling vision, overcame some of the greatest obstacles to mobilize fellow-leaders to fulfill the vision in their lifetimes. We will be no wiser than the teachers we learn from. I encourage you to purchase this powerful read for yourself and become a wise-steward of your vision in the days to come.

Dr. Leonard Sweet
Best Selling Author & Futurist
Drew Theological School, Tabor College, George Fox University

Bishop Ulmer's revelatory insight into the scriptures flows from the heart of God. Bishop Ulmer's life is a legacy of excellence, integrity, and visionary leadership, impacting and lifting the next generation. *The Forgotten Baptism*; the baptism into leadership, awakens us to authentic leadership and vision in this journey together.

Bishop Robert Stearns
The Tabernacle, Buffalo NY
Executive Director, Eagles' Wings

I have long believed that the present-day Church didn't have a preaching, teaching, singing or facilities problem, it has a leadership problem. The weak link in God's desire to establish His Kingdom on earth as it is in heaven is leadership! Leadership is *The Forgotten Baptism*. There is no one more qualified to address this BIG Kingdom Issue than Dr. Kenneth C. Ulmer. Dr. Ulmer is one of the rare voices who has navigated the minefield of leadership with success and integrity for well over 30 years. He is a leader's leader and has spent most of his life helping leaders at every level win. This book is a fountain that flows from his global perspective, wisdom and heart for God's agenda. This book will help you become who you are called to be, so you can do what needs to be done and do what the world is waiting for...Lead!

Van Moody
Bestselling Author The People Factor & The I-Factor
Founder of The Leadership Institute

Nothing of true lasting value happens without intentional, careful, proactive leadership. I've been humbled to look through the rearview mirror of my life and see God use me to influence others, but that influence has happened because I sat at the feet of some incredible leaders...leaders like Bishop Ulmer. For over a quarter of a century he has invested deeply in me, and I'm a living witness that what leaks from these pages has spilled out of his life. When it comes to leadership many talk a good game, but few live up to the hype. Bishop Ulmer does.

Bryan Loritts, Senior Pastor,
Abundant Life Christian Fellowship;
Author, Saving the Saved.

THE FORGOTTEN
BAPTISM

YOUR LEADERSHIP PATH TO
FULFILLING YOUR VISION

KENNETH C. ULMER
JAMES O. DAVIS

The Forgotten Baptism –Your Leadership Path to Fulfilling Your Vision
By: Bishop Kenneth C. Ulmer and Dr. James O. Davis

Published by Billion Soul Publishing, Inc.
PO Box 623307
Oviedo, Florida 32762
(407) 563-4806
www.ahigherlife.com

Hardback ISBN 13: 978-0-9978018-3-5
eBook ISBN: 978-0-9989773-5-5

First Edition
13 14 15 16 17 — 12 11 10 9 8 7 6 5
Printed in the United States of America

IN DEDICATION

To our beloved friend,
Dr. Jack Hayford,
who has led us
with vision, valor, and victory!

FOREWORD

As Christian leaders, one of the most important skills we can ever acquire is to see and lead with a God-sized vision. For example, all pastors should shepherd the people of God and have a pastoral spirit, but it takes certain kinds of leaders to be "seers." In the Old Testament, the prophets were called "seers." Why? They could see things other people couldn't see. They saw things hundreds or thousands of years into the future. As Christian leaders, we are supposed to be able to see things as we move our organizations into the future.

God is the initiator of His vision, and the leader becomes the responder to and implementer of God's vision. God initiates the vision himself. We, as leaders, respond to God's visionary initiation. Then, we as visionary leaders are responsible to implement the vision wherever we live, in whatever nation, in whatever society, in whatever culture, in whatever city, and in whatever town we live in. We are responsible to implement the vision that God has already given, not the one we dreamed up.

One of the greatest obstacles in visionary leadership is not only the limited ability to spiritually house God-sized vision, but the ability to baptize our followers into this vision. It's not just what we want to do; it's what God wants to do through us. It is what God has already said He's going to do. When we become a part of God's vison, we are beginning to have a thorough understanding of what the church is, where the church is going, and how to lead others into the baptism of the vision.

God is the author of vision. His nature is to be providential and purposeful. When God created the Earth and the universe, this was brought into reality from nothing but God's Word. Creation progressed from a state of nothingness through a state of formlessness and emptiness to a condition when formlessness gave way to form and emptiness surrendered to fullness. This explains the creation of vision by God. Vision is also created in leaders who carry vision from God.

As we start to envision the future, there's no form, no fullness, and no fruit yet. This is why we are called to become visionary leaders. God has called us to see ahead of time where barrenness can break forth and be fruitful. We can see where nothing will become something.

Other people can't see it, and they might even question what we see, but that is the God piece in leadership that makes us visionary leaders. This is the power of vision at work. Vision turns nothingness and emptiness into something and fulfillment. In Genesis1:1–2, we see how God created the heavens and the Earth. The Earth was without form, and darkness was on the face of the deep until the Spirit of God moved upon them. When the Spirit of God moved upon Earth and the deep, mighty, creative things began to happen!

In *The Forgotten Baptism*, Dr. Kenneth C. Ulmer and Dr. James O. Davis take the reader on the epic leadership journey of a full understanding of what visionary leadership is; how to develop it in our lives; and how to baptize our people, churches, and organizations into the vision that God has given to us. In 1 Corinthians 10:2, we read that "They were all baptized into Moses in the cloud and the sea..." Moses was one of the greatest visionary leaders of all time. God gave him "the vision," and he led his people into the vision.

In *The Forgotten Baptism,* you will learn how to receive a God-sized vision and impart it to everybody around you, making sure all the people are on the same page, walking in the same path, embracing the same values, and walking in unity of heart. If the visionary leader is not able to pass it on and pace it through others, then very few followers will be baptized into the vision.

As you read *The Forgotten Baptism,* your visionary capacity will be enlarged, making it possible for you to see ahead of time and space and to be able to bring your people into God's fullness for their lives. I believe this powerful resource is a must for our generation, as we strive to lead our churches, organizations, and ministries into God's victorious fullness. While we seem to be living at times at "the speed of blur," we need to slow down enough to be powerfully baptized into God's vision for people's lives and to learn how to bring our followers into it. God wants to baptize you into the greatest and grandest vision of your life!

Rev. Robert Morris
Gateway Church
Southlake, Texas (near Dallas)
May 2017

PREFACE

It began in a tightly crowded classroom at St. Anne's College, Oxford University. Dr. Leonard Sweet was teaching on leadership. He ran a short video of a hillside picnic over the beach scene.

In the video, one lone and rather rhythmically spastic but blissfully jovial young man begins to whirl and twirl to the assumed beats of imaginary silent music. (I would learn later that the sound was turned down, and the narrative and background music of the clip were silent.) He is caught up in the revelry of artistic freestyle. After a minute or so, another single observer drifts into the undesignated space of the dancer and begins to mimic the uncoordinated choreography of the original dancer. He quickly copies the movements of the leader and then seemingly begins his own improvisational version that is an identifiable variation of the originator's nonspecific theme.

Now the third person fades in. He seems to be copying both the originator and the first follower. Both the enthusiasm and the instructive display of the leader, which is now on display by the first follower and contagiously spread to the second follower, is picked up by the third. And then, one by one—almost as if being pulled in by some invisible rope—dancer–follower after dancer–follower joins the celebration until the hill is alive with the jigs of dancers. A hillside dance troupe is formed as each participant is merged; immersed, swallowed up into, blended, and, dare I say, "baptized" into the leader.

This scenario sparked my inquisitive mind and led me on a journey of investigation into the dynamics of the relationship between a leader and those whose lives are attached to him or her. In the video I watched, the hillside scene looks like a sinkhole, and one person after another was being absorbed into the vision of that lone dancer. I discovered that there is a model. There is a method. Moses and Israel represent the model. Baptism is the method, the metaphor, and the means that connects leaders and those who join with them. It is a picture we can easily overlook as we peruse the pages of holy writ.

What follows is an investigation and examination of the principle of *leadership baptism*. Don't let that term frighten you. This is not a Sunday School lesson about one of the ancient historical tales of antiquity. It is not a series of ivory-tower platitudes rained down from the heights of intellectualism or theological pontification. Instead, we will dissect and dilute the religious jargon and show you how practical, useful, and adaptable this principle of *leadership baptism* can be for your business, your career, your ministry, and even your life.

In a paraphrase of the formula used in many African American churches during water baptism: "I do indeed baptize you, my friend—in the name of *leadership*!"

TABLE OF CONTENTS

Foreword xiii

Introduction 1

1. The Visionary Pillar 7

2. The Visionary Premise 19

3. The Visionary Person 31

4. The Visionary Process 51

5. The Visionary Problems 67

6. The Visionary Power 87

7. The Visionary Path 107

8. The Visionary Portrait 137

Conclusion 151

About the Authors 157

Bibliography 161

INTRODUCTION

From the beginning of time, visionary leaders have made their definable mark on mankind. There are those who have moved the masses, while others have mobilized the marketplace. Whether these leaders have served in the secular spheres of society or in the sacred arenas of the church, there are undeniable truths that bring them through the tough times and ultimately to fulfillment of their dreams. Only the visionary leader truly knows the pain, the price, and the pleasure of dreams becoming destinies.

We are all familiar with water baptism and Spirit baptism. In 1 Corinthians 10:1–2, we find an interesting baptism that most of us have never heard of or studied in our lives. We suggest that it is the *forgotten baptism*, or *leadership baptism*. The Bible says that they were all baptized—placed into or immersed into Moses. They were immersed, positioned, into Moses. This is not Spirit baptism. This is not water baptism. We suggest that it is the baptism into *servant leadership*. That exemplary form of leadership for the visionary leaders of our churches is the focus of this book.

The late Dr. Jerry Falwell, cofounder of Liberty University and founder of Thomas Road Baptist Church in Lynchburg, Virginia, repeatedly shared the five questions that caused him to see visions and to dream dreams. We believe visionary leaders ask and answer these same five questions. Here is the first one:

- What is it that you really hope to accomplish with your life?

When a student attends Harvard Business School, he or she will be asked a similar question: "What is your BHAG—your big, hairy, audacious goal? Write down your BHAG for life, and forty years from now, look at it to see how you did."

Here are the other four questions Dr. Falwell shared and that we ask visionary leaders to ask and answer:

- What would I try to do if I thought I might succeed?
- What goals would I set if I knew I could not fail?
- What price am I willing to pay?
- What sacrifices am I willing to make?

If you desire to become a visionary leader who impacts your family, your ministry, and your world, then you will have to ask and answer these five questions over and over again.[1]

The key vision verse in the Bible is Proverbs 29:18: "Where there is no vision the people perish. But he that keeps the law, happy is he."

What Is Vision?

What is vision? Vision is a bridge from the past to the future. How do I get from where I am right now to where God

---

[1] Falwell, Jerry L. Vision: An Artistic Message. Beyond All Limits Conference. Orlando, Florida 2004.

wants me to be tomorrow? We can accomplish this only by dreaming dreams and seeing visions and then making ourselves available to God, who will equip us to implement those visions.[2]

What is vision? Vision is the eye of faith to see the invisible and the decisiveness to make it become visible. Visionary leaders can see buildings before they are built. They can see across the landscape of time and see what is coming their way. Vision is the power that causes people to make huge sacrifices to become all they can become for God.

Christian futurist George Barna said vision is a *clear mental image of a preferable future* imparted by God to His chosen servants and that it is based on an accurate understanding of God's self and circumstances.[3] Think about those words: "A clear mental image of a preferable future." If you could make a wish right now—if you could summarize in a couple of sentences what you'd like to be ten, twenty, thirty, or forty years from now, what would that statement be?

Vision is also the ability to adopt an action plan that will enable you to move forward in your Christian life and ministry. You must not just dream a dream. You need an action plan. We can't just dream; we've got to do. This means we have to get up early every morning. This means we probably have to stop going to all the seminars and meetings and get started putting in our time to bring the vision to reality.

Vision is the inward fire that enables you to boldly communicate to your peers what the future will be like. It's not enough just to get a vision. You must be able to pass it on to your children, mom, dad, grandparent, church, and organization. When God sets your soul on fire, you've got to learn how artistically to communicate that to every member of

---

[2] Towns, Elmer. "Casting Vision And Mobilizing Leaders", Global Church Learning Center. 2014

[3] Barna, George. *The Power of Vision*. Regal Books, 2009. P.23.

your organization. We should strive get our people fired up to the point that they'll charge hell for the bucket of water![4]

Vision is the dynamic that enables you to translate your faith and dreams into a new and personal walk with God. Vision is the dynamic that leads you into a powerful, personal walk with Him. Vision is the God-given energy that will make you become a risk taker. This is what separates the men from the boys at critical times in life.

Standing upon Our Watch

We have been on the edge of ruin so many times that it is boring when things are going nicely! Crises ought to motivate us, drive us to the closet of prayer. May the Lord help you to learn how to step out in faith. We are convinced that unless we are constantly attempting greater things and reaching out for the impossible, the supernatural, then we really are not men and women of vision.

Habakkuk 2:1–2 says, "I will stand upon my watch, and set me upon the tower, and will watch to see what he will say unto me, and what I shall answer when I am reproved. And the LORD answered me, and said, 'Write the vision, and make *it* plain upon tables, that he may run that readeth it.'

What is your "watch"? Our watch is our role in our ministry to this generation. This is what our Lord has called us to be and do. Do you know what your role is in God's goal for this generation?

"And set me upon the tower," Habakkuk said. "The tower" is our personal relationship with Him—where we dream the dreams and see the visions by contacting Him on a daily basis.

---

[4] Falwell, Jerry L. "Vision: An Artistic Message." Beyond All Limits Conference, Orlando, Florida. 2004

Next Habakkuk says, "I will watch to see what he (God) will say unto me, and what I shall answer when I am reproved." What the Lord is saying to you and me is, "Write the vision, and make it plain upon tables, that he may run that reads it."

This means we need to get our people so energized that they can't wait for church to get over, to go out and tell people how to be saved, to go out and build the church, to go out to the mission field, to go out on a short-term mission trip, or whatever God has stirred their hearts to do. We must be baptized in leadership.

Then Habakkuk writes in verses 3 and 4, "For the vision is yet for an appointed time, but at the end it shall speak, and not lie: though it tarry, wait for it; because it will surely come, it will not tarry. Behold, his soul which is lifted up as not upright in him: but the just shall live by his faith."

Start dreaming dreams. Start reaching out to God for great and glorious things. Get a BHAG that is so large, it will make your deacons nervous! God is looking for men and women who will dare to challenge Him by the magnitude of their visions. When we cast our vision to the stars, it will mostly likely land on the moon. If we, however, cast our vision to the trees, it will most likely hit the ground!

Honoring God with the Magnitude of Our Requests

Napoleon was a dreamer. He and his generals, who were in search of world conquests, were quite surprised on one occasion. They encountered unexpected resistance while attempting to capture an island in the Mediterranean. They encountered much bloodshed and lost some of their best men. They were finally victorious.

As was his custom, the emperor brought his generals around the table for a feast of celebration. While they were sitting there, a young, brash officer approached the emperor, a move that could be fatal without an invitation. The emperor looked up and said words that must have struck fear into Napoleon's heart: "What do you want?" The generals were incensed that he would dare to insult the emperor with such presumption.

The young officer said, "Sir, please give me this island."

That absolutely irritated the generals to the degree they were about to stand and arrest him. But the emperor asked for paper and a pencil, wrote out a deed to the island, and promptly gave it to Napoleon.

The response from the generals was expected: "Sir, how could you do such a thing? We paid an awesome price. How could you do that?"

His answer was, "The young man honored me with the magnitude of his request."

We need to begin honoring God with the magnitude of our requests. We need to begin believing that he is the eternal God; that nothing is too hard for him. Dare God to do through you what not even your spouse believes is possible, not even your family can believe it when it happens. God is looking for dreamers with this artistic message who will dare to see visions, dream dreams, and do the impossible.

We wrote *The Forgotten Baptism* for visionaries and dreamers who want to follow Almighty God's plan to use their lives to genuinely transform their families, their organizations, and their respective worlds. As you read this timely book, you will feel the fires of faith and at times smell the fuel of frustration that eventually comes to every visionary leader. Prepare to get baptized in leadership!

CHAPTER 1

THE VISIONARY PILLAR

Churches have split. Denominations have been formed, have died, and have been rebirthed just over the issue of baptism. The issue of baptism has caused divisions, debates, discussions, schisms, and isms that should be wassums in the Body of Christ. The two-most common baptisms in the church are water baptism and Spirit baptism. Water baptism is a "faith baptism," and Spirit baptism is a "fire baptism."

Why do we call water baptism the "visionary pillar"? We must lay the foundation of our faith properly before we can build our visionary house. If we are going to dream God-sized dreams and see God-sized visions, we believe first and foremost that we must know God intimately and have a vibrant, personal relationship with Him. There is one place where the Lord will not work—in second place. Jesus did not conquer death, hell, and the grave to *have* a place in our hearts; He wants to *be* a place in our hearts.

Before we can genuinely cast a God-sized vision and mobilize our people to follow us in this vision—before we can be baptized in leadership—we must identify ourselves with Christ and know Him on a firsthand basis every day. We cannot teach people what we do not know and lead them where we have never been by ourselves. We must be baptized into the vision that God has given to us before we can truly lead others into this same baptism. Just as Jesus became our example by being baptized in water, we must follow Him as His disciples. In the same manner, we demonstrate to our churches, people, or organizations that we have been baptized into "the vision" and are now prepared to show them how to experience this visionary baptism in their lives. Just as faith is required for water baptism to make a difference in our lives and for us to be identified with Christ and Him with us; faith is a nonnegotiable pillar on the path to successfully implementing a God-sized vision in our lives.

Three Elements of Water Baptism

There are at least three elements of every water baptism:

1. The baptizer—the person who is doing the baptism. In many cases, it's a minister.
2. The person being baptized—let's call him or her the "baptizee."
3. Some element that the person will be baptized into—in this case, it is water.

In other words, somebody baptizes a person into something. The baptizer baptizes the baptizee into the element of water.

There are several issues about baptism that probably will not be resolved on this side of heaven. For example, we will not have consensus on church policy, including the role of elders, presbytery, and pastoral authority. We won't agree on that. Also, women in ministry—what can women do? What positions are exclusively for men? Does God call women to preach? We won't solve that. The church will probably never agree on water baptism. No two organizations do it the same way. Do you sprinkle the baptizees with water? Do you pour water over them, or do you dunk them? And if you dunk them, how many times do you dunk them? And when you dunk them, do you dunk them forward, or do you dunk them backward? What do you say when you dunk them? Do you baptize them in the name of the Father, the name of the Son, and the name of the Holy Ghost, or do you baptize them in the name of Jesus? The global church does not agree on any of this.

Even though this book does not even remotely attempt to try to solve the differences that organizations have regarding water baptism, this baptism does help lay the foundation for the "forgotten baptism." We believe every visionary leader will need to fulfill the vision that God has placed in his or her heart.

> We believe every visionary leader will need to fulfill the vision that God has placed in his or her heart.

The teaching of water baptism begins with the baptism of Jesus. Jesus commenced his public ministry by being baptized in water. The greatest visionary leader of all generations was baptized in water.

How did Jesus conclude His ministry? He commanded us to go into all the world and baptize people in the name of the Father, the Son, and the Holy Ghost. He commenced and concluded his ministry by putting a pointed emphasis on water baptism.

His ministry lasted only about three and a half years. The Gospel of Mark particularly reveals that the public ministry of Jesus began with Him being baptized in water. Mark 1 tells the story of Jesus, including his baptism.

Preparation for Baptism

An important component of baptism is *the preparation for baptism*.

Who is prepared to be baptized? How do you prepare yourself for baptism? What is the prerequisite for Bible baptism?

Is it the "good news" that prepares us for water baptism? The apostle Mark states in Mark 1:1, "The beginning of the gospel of Jesus Christ the Son of God. As it is written in the prophets, 'Behold, I send my messenger before thy face, which shall prepare thy way before me.' That was a prophecy concerning John the Baptist: "...which shall prepare thy way before me."

Be sure to underscore the word "prepare." "The voice of one crying in the wilderness, 'Prepare ye the word of the Lord. Make his paths straight. John did baptize in the wilderness and preach the baptism of repentance for the remission of sins.' "

The word used in this text for "prepare" is an interesting one from a historical standpoint. It was used particularly to speak of the traditional manner in which kings would journey from one place to another. In ancient times, when a king and eastern monarch would get ready to go somewhere they didn't want him to be inconvenienced at all and so what they would do would be to prepare a road. They would build a special road for him: And they would fill in the low places. They would level-off the high places. And they would straighten out the crooked places so this eastern monarch would just have an easy journey. Metaphorically it was an appropriate word when it referred to the coming king, the Messiah, Jesus the Christ.

Preparing for Baptism through Repentance and Faith

Now, John says we had better prepare like that for the coming of the Lord. Our Lord is going to come like that to the deserts of our lives, the wilderness of our lives. And we need to make a road for royalty; we need to prepare the way of the Lord. We need to have a bulldozer that will straighten things out and make things ready for the coming of the Lord. That bulldozer is repentance.

Repentance: What does it do? It brings down mountains of pride. It fills up valleys of failure. It straightens out the crooked places of deceit. It makes a road through which the Lord comes into the wilderness and the parched desert of our lives, to bring His reviving power. John said baptism is the outward sign that we have repented. The preparation for baptism is repentance. Repentance is not incidental; it is fundamental.

What did Jesus preach? In Mark 1:14–15, we read, "Now after that John was put into prison, Jesus came into Galilee, preaching the gospel of the kingdom of God. And saying, 'The time is fulfilled, and the kingdom of God is at hand: repent ye, and believe the gospel.' " Repentance and faith are the keys to preparation for water baptism.

Repentance and faith are heads and tails of the same coin. When the Bible says "faith," it infers repentance. And when it says repentance it infers faith. When you turn from sin you turn to God. When you turn to God you turn from sin. That's the reason that repentance and faith are heads and tails of the same coin.[5]

On the heels of the preparation of baptism is the *proclamation of baptism*.

The Proclamation of Baptism

What does baptism proclaim? How do you envision it? This brings up a very interesting point. We said that repentance is preparation for baptism. Why, then, was Jesus baptized? He did not have anything to repent of. When John saw Jesus coming, John said, "I have need to be baptized of thee, and comest thou to me?" (Matt. 3:14) John is telling Jesus that He should be baptizing John, not the other way around. In Matthew 3:11, John says, "I indeed baptize you with water unto repentance: but he that cometh after me is mightier than

---

5   MacArthur, John. New Testament Commentary. Mark 1-8. Moody Publishers. 2015. pp. 11-24.

I, whose shoes I am not worthy to bear: he shall baptize you with the Holy Ghost, and *with* fire..." Today John might say, "I'm not even worthy to get down and untie Your shoelaces, but You want me to baptize You?"

Do you know who John the Baptist was? He was a cousin of Jesus. They were born about the same time, and they grew up together. If Jesus had been a sinner, who would have known it? John would have known it. If you can't say something bad about your kinfolks, whom can you say something bad about?

Jesus wasn't a sinner. As a matter of fact, God said of the glory of the baptism of Jesus, "This is my beloved Son in whom I am well pleased" (Matt. 3:17). He wasn't a sinner. He was the Son of God. Why, then, was Jesus baptized? It has a lot to do with why we are baptized. "Baptism" has a lot to do with identification.

> If you can't say something bad about your kinfolks, whom can you say something bad about?

When Jesus was baptized, He was identifying Himself with us. When we are baptized, we are identifying ourselves with Him. There is a very real sense in which we meet Jesus in the water of baptism. Jesus came to take our place.

He came to take our place. He was our substitute. There was a mortgage against us that we could not pay. When Jesus was baptized, He was signing His name to that mortgage and saying, in essence, "I will pay in full. I am identifying myself with these people I have come to save. I am not a sinner, but I am identifying myself with these people." And it was a fore-shadowing of the coming death, burial, and resurrection of Jesus Christ.[6]

His death had our names on it. When Jesus died, He died for us. When He rose, we rose with Him. That's what baptism means. It represents His sacrifice and our salvation because

---

[6] MacArthur, John. New Testament Commentary. Mark 1-8. Moody Publishers. 2015. pp. 27-38.

we are identified with the Lord. We have been saved. Water baptism also signifies that when Jesus comes again, just like we came out of that water, we are going to come out of our graves.

There is a story about two caterpillars that were crawling around the ground and saw a butterfly flying toward them. One caterpillar said to the other one, "You couldn't get me up in one of those things for a million dollars." In the future, we are going to "get up in one of those things"! We are down here now groveling on this Earth, but one of these days, a great transformation is going to come when we are caught up to be like our Lord. This is the proclamation of baptism—the death, burial, and resurrection of Jesus Christ.

Visionary Leader Spotlight: Martin Luther

One of the greatest faith visionaries of all time was the Protestant reformer, Martin Luther.

On October 31, 1517, Martin Luther posted a list of questions and propositions for debate that he had written, titled "Ninety-Five Theses," on the door of the Castle Church in Wittenberg, Germany. The document is also known by the title "Disputation on the Power and Efficacy of Indulgences." This began the second greatest event in the church since the Day of Pentecost. From the time he first began to question church authority to when he nailed the theses to those doors, he had only wanted answers. When no answers were forthcoming, he tried to drive the church to reform, and when that was rebuked, he stripped the church's authority over him. His protest for reform challenged countless others to do likewise.

His actions, in turn, sparked not only a call for reform but a demand for religious and spiritual changes throughout Europe. In fact, it sparked the Protestant Reformation.

Born in Eisleben, Germany, in 1483, Martin Luther went on to become one of Western history's most significant figures. Luther spent his early years in relative anonymity as a monk and scholar. But in 1517, Luther penned the "Ninety-Five Theses" document attacking the Catholic Church's corrupt practice of selling "indulgences" to absolve sin. The document presented two central beliefs: that the Bible is the central religious authority and that humans may reach salvation only by their faith, not by their deeds. Although these ideas had been advanced before, Martin Luther codified them at a moment in history that was ripe for religious reformation. The Catholic Church was ever-after divided, and the Protestantism that soon emerged was shaped by Luther's ideas. His writings changed the course of religious and cultural history in the West.[7]

Luther's father was a prosperous businessman, and when Luther was young, his father moved the family of ten to Mansfeld. At age five, Luther began his education at a local school, where he learned reading, writing, and Latin. At thirteen, Luther began to attend a school run by the Brethren of the Common Life in Magdeburg. The Brethren's teachings focused on personal piety, and while there, Luther developed an early interest in monastic life.

Luther began to live the spartan and rigorous life of a monk but did not abandon his studies. Between 1507 and 1510, he studied at the University of Erfurt and at a university in Wittenberg. In 1510–11, he took a break from his education to serve as a representative in Rome for the German Augustinian monasteries. In 1512, Luther received his doctorate and became a professor of biblical studies. Over the next five years, his continuing theological studies would lead him to insights that would have implications for Christian thought for centuries to come.

---

[7] Hillerbrand, Hans J. Martin Luther: German Religious Leader. Encyclopedia Britannica. January, 24, 2017. www/Britannica.com/biography/Martin-Luther.

In early sixteenth-century Europe, some theologians and scholars were beginning to question the teachings of the Roman Catholic Church. It was also around this time that translations of original texts—namely, the Bible and the writings of the early church philosopher Augustine—became more widely available. Augustine (340–430) had emphasized the primacy of the Bible rather than church officials as the ultimate religious authority. He also believed that humans could not reach salvation by their own acts, but that only God could bestow salvation by His divine grace. In the Middle Ages, the Catholic Church taught that salvation was possible through "good works," or works of righteousness, that pleased God. Luther came to share Augustine's two central beliefs, which would later form the basis of Protestantism.

Meanwhile, the Catholic Church's practice of granting "indulgences" to provide absolution to sinners became increasingly corrupt. Indulgence selling had been banned in Germany, but the practice continued unabated. In 1517, a friar named Johann Tetzel began to sell indulgences in Germany to raise funds to renovate St. Peter's Basilica in Rome. Committed to the idea that salvation could be reached through faith and by divine grace only, Luther vigorously objected to the corrupt practice of selling indulgences. This is when he wrote the "The Ninety-Five Theses" and defiantly nailed the document to the door of the Wittenberg Castle church. The reality was probably not so dramatic; Luther more likely hung the document on the door of the church matter-of-factly to announce the ensuing academic discussion around it that he was organizing.

"The Ninety-Five Theses," which would later become the foundation of the Protestant Reformation, were written in a remarkably humble and academic tone, questioning rather than accusing. The overall thrust of the document was nonetheless quite provocative. The first two theses contained Luther's central idea—that God intended believers to seek repentance and that faith alone, and not deeds, would lead to salvation. The other ninety-three theses, a number of them directly criticizing the practice of indulgences, supported the first two.

The document was quickly distributed throughout Germany and then made its way to Rome. In 1518, Luther was summoned to Augsburg, a city in southern Germany, to defend his opinions before an imperial diet (assembly). A debate lasting three days between Luther and Cardinal Thomas Cajetan produced no agreement. Cajetan defended the church's use of indulgences, but Luther refused to recant, and he returned to Wittenberg.

On November 9, 1518, the pope condemned Luther's writings as conflicting with the teachings of the church. One year later, a series of commissions were convened to examine Luther's teachings. The first papal commission found them to be heretical, but the second merely stated that Luther's writings were "scandalous and offensive to pious ears." Finally, in July 1520, Pope Leo X issued a papal bull (public decree) concluding that Luther's propositions were heretical and gave Luther 120 days to recant in Rome. Luther refused to recant, and on January 3, 1521, Pope Leo excommunicated Martin Luther from the Catholic Church.[8]

"Here I stand. God help me. I can do no other."

On April 17, 1521, Luther appeared before the Diet of Worms in Germany. Refusing again to recant, he concluded his testimony with this defiant statement: "Here I stand. God help me. I can do no other." On May 25, the Holy Roman emperor Charles V signed an edict against Luther, ordering his writings to be burned. Luther hid in the town of Eisenach for the next year, where he began work on one of his major

[8] English Bible History. Greatsite.com/English-bible-history/martin-luther.html.

life projects—the translation of the New Testament into German, which took him ten years to complete.

Luther returned to Wittenberg in 1521, where the reform movement initiated by his writings had grown beyond his influence. Martin Luther is one of the most influential figures in Western history. His writings were responsible for fractionalizing the Catholic Church and sparking the Protestant Reformation. He was first baptized into the God-revealed insights and then was able to lead the people from where they were to a new and vibrant relationship with Christ. His central teachings—that the Bible is the central source of religious authority and that salvation is reached through faith, not deeds—shaped the core of Protestantism. Although Luther was critical of the Catholic Church, he distanced himself from the radical successors who took up his mantle. Some of Luther's most significant contributions to theological history, however, were truly revolutionary in his day—such as his insistence that as the sole source of religious authority the Bible be translated and made available to everyone.[9]

The Protestant Reformation would change Christianity forever from a religion with one omnipotent power, the Catholic Church, to encompass myriad new beliefs using a separate Protestant context. That context is based on differing scriptural interpretations, not only different from that of the Roman Catholic Church, but in many instances, different from one another. This pluralism has continued to this day and can be found in the great number of denominations within Protestantism, and those that stand outside that framework as well. All modern-day Christian streams have as their fountainhead the Protestant Reformation that began in Wittenberg, Germany.

---

[9] Marty, Martin E. *Christianity Today*. Christianitytoday.com/history/theologians/
martin-luther.html.

THE FORGOTTEN BAPTISM

CHAPTER 2

THE VISIONARY PREMISE

There have been a lot of scriptural and spiritual conflicts over Spirit baptism. If you thought the ecclesiastical battles were terrible over water baptism, the Spirit baptism struggles go to the next level and beyond!

The theological arguments usually center around *glossolalia* (speaking in tongues) and around whether this phenomenon is for today or ceased at the close of the early church period. Church leaders from certain denominations have called those who speak in tongues devil-inspired, ignorant, or immature Christians and false teachers.

Arguments also center around when do you do it, when do you get it, and what do you do when you get it? And do I have to do what I do and you do what you did when you got it? And what do I have to say, or do I have to say anything, when I get it? And do I get it before? Do I get it after? We don't agree on Spirit baptism, either.

Just as water baptism symbolizes "the faith," or the entrance into the visionary life with Christ, Spirit baptism is "the fire," or the empowerment of the visionary life for Christ. With this being articulated, we desperately need to recognize that God has a purpose and a power for His visionary leaders. There has never been a greater day, a greater age, in which to preach and teach the glorious Gospel of our Lord and Savior Jesus Christ than in this day and age.

Our *mandate* has not changed. The Lord Jesus has never withdrawn the Great Commission. It is just as powerful, just as real, today as it ever has been.

Not only has our mandate not changed; our *Master* has not changed. Jesus Christ is the same yesterday, today, and forever. He is not getting old, and He's not sick. Jesus has as much power in the twenty-first century as he had in the first century.

Our mandate has not changed, our Master has not changed, and our *message* has not changed. We don't need a new and a modern Gospel for a new and modern age.

Yet *mankind* has continued to change. Men and women have become so hard and wicked in this

> Our mandate has not changed, our Master has not changed, and our *message* has not changed. We don't need a new and a modern Gospel for a new and modern age.

generation. Adam was totally depraved, and you can't get worse than that. God has never had anything but sinners to work with. Concerning all the wickedness that's on the outside, 1 John 4:4 says, "Greater is he that is in you," (that is the Holy Spirit) "than he that is in the world"—that's the devil.

Principles of Power for Leaders to Follow

There are principles of power for us to follow. We believe every visionary leader not only needs a baptism of faith but a baptism of fire in their ministries. This leads to leadership baptism. Acts 2:1–4 says, "And when the day of Pentecost was fully come, they were all in one accord in one place. And suddenly there came a sound from heaven as of a mighty rushing wind, and it filled all the house where they were sitting. And there appeared unto them cloven tongues like as of fire, and it sat upon each of them. And they were all filled with the Holy Spirit and began to speak with other tongues, as the Spirit gave them utterance."

Pentecost was a special feast day in the life of Israel. The Israelites had been keeping this feast for fifteen hundred years, but this one was special. Luke, the author of the book of Acts, states, "And when the day of Pentecost was fully come, they were all together in one place" (Acts 2:1). In other words, in the past, it had come and gone each year for fifteen hundred years, but now it had come to stay.

When we review the Day of Pentecost in the book of Acts, we note that this God-given power was *symbolized* through "wind" and "fire." There was a sound, and there was a sight. The sound was a like a rushing, powerful tornado. But this one was not outside the house; it was inside the house! Luke says there was a "sound" of a mighty wind. There was no wind, just the *sound* of wind. I smile when I see pictures of the Day of Pentecost that depict the scene with torrents of wind or swirling, smoky waves of fire swirling or blowing in the same direction. They heard the sound of wind without being "blown away" (no pun intended). Just as the wind is invisible, indispensable, and unpredictable, so is the Holy Spirit in our lives and in the world, today.

Also, the Holy Spirit was symbolized by fire. In Acts 2:3, we read, "And there appeared unto them cloven tongues like as of fire, and it sat upon each of them." They looked like 120 human candles. God sparked the flame of the Holy Spirit and spread it by His sovereign wind!

This power was not only symbolized; it also was *vocalized*. "And they were all filled with the Holy Ghost, and began to speak with other tongues, as the Spirit gave them utterance" (Acts 2:4). There were 120 people now beginning to speak in languages unknown to them but known to others who heard them speak.

This power was not only symbolized and vocalized; it also was *actualized*. The Bible says they were all filled with the

Holy Spirit. The abiding principle is the fullness of the Holy Spirit. The abiding miracle of Pentecost is that men, women, and young people can be filled with the Holy Spirit.

With the baptism of fire, there are three major principles of power for visionary leaders. Without this God-given power, visons will not be victories, and dreams will not become destinies. The Holy Spirit is a *promise to be received*.

In Acts: 2:39, "For the promise is unto you and to your children, to all that are far off, even as many as the Lord our God shall call." God has made a promise to you. Luke does not say, "This promise was for you;" but he said, "This promise is for you." In other words, this promise is for today!

> God doesn't want us to have the Holy Spirit in us, just as a residing person. He wants that power to be released in our hearts, lives, and ministries. We can claim that power through leadership baptism.

The second principle is the Holy Spirit is a *power to be released*. In Acts 1:8: "You shall receive power after that the Holy Spirit is come upon you." You shall receive *dunamis*, a dynamic power will be in you.

God wants us to live with power. God doesn't want us to have the Holy Spirit in us, just as a residing person. He wants that power to be released in our hearts, lives, and ministries. We can claim that power through leadership baptism.

Christ Is the Way to Holiness

One of the greatest things we have learned in life is that holiness is not the way to Christ; Christ is the way to holiness. We hope you can understand this. It doesn't mean you can come, wanting to be filled with the Holy Spirit, with your heart full of sin. No! Peter said we must repent. But please don't think you can *earn* anything from God. The power of the Holy Spirit is a gift. We need to quit trying to make ourselves worthy and start trusting in the promises of God. We are not worthy by ourselves for any of the gifts from God.

Because the Holy Spirit of God is a promise to be received, then He is a power to be released. So why are we so pathetic? Why are there so many in church, yet we're doing so little? We have not allowed the Holy Spirit of God to do what He wants to do in our hearts and in our lives.

On the Day of Pentecost, 3,000 people got saved through 120 witnesses. Today we can have 3,000 witnesses and not see 120 saved in a year! What's the difference? Well, the difference is that we're trying to do it in our own power rather than depending upon the Holy Spirit of God. One of the greatest deficiencies in the contemporary church is the lack of authentic spiritual power that changes lives. A powerless pulpit is often camouflaged by high-tech aesthetics and highly polished artistic skill that all too often reduces spiritual congregations to impotent audiences that are more impressed than improved. They leave feeling better but not living better.

The presence and power of the Holy Spirit is not an additional optional extra but the very essence of a life lived in relationship to Jesus, who was anointed by the same Holy Spirit that would resurrect Him from the damp grave on the other side of Calvary. If the Son of the Living God lived in the anointing of the Holy Spirit, how much more do we likewise need that same power! God the Father so loves us that He makes available to us the very same Holy Spirit power that raised Jesus the Son from the grave. He, the Holy Spirit, is truly a power to be released.

The Holy Spirit is a promise to be received, a power to be released, and *a person to be recognized*. On the Day of Pentecost, they saw all of this and asked, "What does all of this mean?"

Acts 2:12–18 says this: And they were all amazed, and were in doubt, saying one to another, "What meaneth this?" Others mocking said, these men are full of new wine. But Peter, having stood up with the eleven, lifted up his voice, and said unto them, "Ye men of Judea, and all ye that dwell at Jerusalem, be this known unto you, and hearken to my words: "For these are not drunken, as ye suppose, seeing it is but the third hour of the day. But this is that which was spoken by the prophet Joel. 'And it shall come to pass in the last days,' saith God, 'I will pour out my Spirit upon all flesh; and your sons and your daughters shall prophesy, and your young men shall see visions, and your old men shall dream dreams. And on my servants and on my hand-maidens I will pour out in those days of my Spirit; and they shall prophesy...' "

Do you know one of the things that kills some churches or organizations? When God starts working, and people start taking credit for it. When we start taking credit for what God does, it stops. What is there about any church that you cannot explain apart from the Holy Spirit of God? Nothing.

> **God doesn't call us to be amusing but amazing.**

When we choose to serve through the power of the Holy Spirit, three responses are common:

Some will be *amazed*. We want the church to be an amazement to people. We want our lives to be an amazement to people. God doesn't call us to be amusing but amazing.

There will be also *amusement*. Verse 13 says, "Others mocking said, these men are full of new wine." When was the last time anybody accused you of being drunk because

24

of your faith or because of your empowerment? When was the last time you were so different that somebody said, "Well, there's something possessing that person"? You know, a person filled with wine—his walk is talk, his walk is changed, his talk is changed, his very demeanor is changed. When we begin to amaze some, we're going to amuse others. They're going to look at us and call us all kinds of names.

And there will be *acknowledgement*. Acts 2:41 says, "Then they that gladly received his word were baptized: and the same day there were added unto them about three thousand souls." There are going to be those who acknowledge Christ as Lord and Savior. We are not talking about wildfire; we are talking about spiritual reality—without which we will not reach this world.

Visionary Leader Spotlight: Adoniram Judson

We close this chapter with one of greatest visionary, missionary stories of all time. We trust it will inspire you to finish what the Lord has chosen for you to be and do in this life. In 1812, Adoniram Judson left Massachusetts for India with his wife, Ann, to become the "First North American Missionary." Here are the actual words of Missionary Judson:

> One day I found a book in the seminary library that talked about a British officer who was sent to Burma in 1795. As I read about the land of Burma where people worshiped idols, I felt a strange fiery excitement inside.
>
> "I am staring at my future!" I thought. "I'll tell the Burmese people about Jesus!"

On February 18, 1812, shortly after I was ordained as a missionary, my new wife Ann and I sailed away from our family and friends in America. Four of my friends became missionaries with us and, in fact, we became known as America's first missionaries. While our friends went to India, Ann and I followed our hearts to Burma, where we hoped to tell the Burmese about Jesus.

After we arrived in Burma, Ann and I learned the new language. It took me years to do it, but I translated the entire Bible into Burmese. Although we told them about Jesus all the time, it took six years before one person accepted Jesus as their Savior.

After a brief stay in India, he and his wife traveled to Burma, arriving in 1813. They were both twenty-four years of age when they left America. In Burma, no one knew the English language, and the Judsons learned the Burmese language on their own.

In those early years, they experienced the heartbreaking loss of two children. In 1822, Ann's health broke, and she returned to the States for rest, publishing a book about their pioneering missionary work in Burma. Upon her return in 1824, Adoniram was imprisoned and tortured. Ann followed her husband from prison to prison and preserved his and several others' lives by bribing officials and providing food.[10]

In 1826, after two years of imprisonment, Adoniram was released. But in October of that same year, while Adoniram was away, Ann died at age thirty-eight, worn out from hardship.

Almost as if he had foreseen her early demise, Adoniram had written this letter to Ann's father years earlier, when he had requested her hand in marriage:

---

[10] Adoniram Judson. Wikipedia.

I have now to ask whether you can consent to part with your daughter early next spring, to see her no more in this world. Whether you can consent to see her departure to a heathen land, and her subjection to the hardships and sufferings of a missionary life? Whether you can consent to her exposure to the dangers of the ocean; to the fatal influence of the southern climate of India; to every kind of want and distress; to the degradation, insult, persecution, and perhaps a violent death? Can you consent to this, for the sake of the perish immortal souls, for the sake of Zion and the glory of God? Can you consent to all this, in hope of soon meeting your daughter in the world of glory, with a crown of righteousness brightened by the acclamations of praise which shall redound to her Savior from heathens saved, through her means, from eternal woe and despair?[11]

Adoniram acclimated to some Burmese customs and built a *zayat*, the customary bamboo and thatch reception shelter, on the street near his home as a reception room and meeting place for Burmese men. Fifteen men attended his first public meeting in April 1819. He was encouraged but suspected that they had come more out of curiosity than anything else. Their attention wandered, and they soon seemed uninterested. Two months later, he baptized his first Burmese convert, Maung Naw, a thirty-five-year-old timber worker from the hill tribes.

It took Judson twelve years to make eighteen converts. Nevertheless, there was much to encourage him. He had written a grammar of the language that is still in use today and

[11] Davis, James O. *Scaling Your Everest: Lessons Learned from Sir Edmund Hillary*. Page 112. 2013.

had begun to translate the Bible. His wife, Ann, was even more fluent in the spoken language of the people than her more academically literate husband. She befriended the wife of the viceroy of Rangoon, as quickly as she did illiterate workers and women.[12]

The essence of Judson's preaching was a combination of conviction of the truth with the rationality of the Christian faith, a firm belief in the authority of the Bible, and a determination to make Christianity relevant to the Burmese mind without violating the integrity of Christian truth, or as he put it, "to preach the gospel, not anti-Buddhism."

By 1823, ten years after his arrival, membership of the little church had grown to 18, and Judson had finally finished the first draft of his translation of the entire text of the New Testament in Burmese.

Judson compiled the first ever Burmese–English dictionary; missionary E. A. Steven completed the English–Burmese half. Every dictionary and grammar written in Burma in the past two centuries has been based on dictionaries originally created by Judson. Judson became a symbol of the preeminence of Bible translation for Protestant missionaries. His translation remains the most popular version in Myanmar. Statistics are not clear, but it seems that there were between 7,000 and 8,000 baptized Burmese converts at the time of Judson's death in 1850. Judson built more than 100 congregations, worked with 163 missionaries in Burma, and completed a Burmese Bible translation! To this day, more than 160 years later, his Burmese Bible translation is still in use.[13]

Adoniram completed an important mission—the Burmese had the Bible in their own language. This translation stands

---

[12] "Adoniram Judson, First Missionary from the United States." http://www.christianity.com/church/church-history/church-history-for-kids/adoniram-judson-first-missionary-from-the-united-states-11635044.html.

[13] Adoniram Judson, First Missionary from the United States. Chrisitianity.com

to this day and is used by more than two million Christians in Myanmar! On April 12, 1850, when Judson was sixty-two years old, he lost his life at sea in the Bay of Bengal.

Each July, Baptist churches in Myanmar celebrate "Judson Day," commemorating his arrival as a missionary. Inside the campus of Yangon University is Judson Church, named in his honor. In 1920 Judson College, named in his honor, merged into Rangoon College, which has since been renamed the University of Rangon. It is located in Yangon, Myanmar.

The American University named in his honor, Judson University was founded in Elgin, Illinois, in 1963. The liberal arts Judson College was separated from the Northern Baptist Theological Seminary, which moved from Chicago to Lombard, Illinois. This American Judson College became Judson University in 2007 and now also has a campus in Rockford, Illinois.

> "Suffering and success go together. If you are succeeding without suffering, it is because others before you have suffered; if you are suffering without succeeding, it is that others after you may succeed."

Judson is honored with a feast day on the liturgical calendar of the Episcopal Church (USA) on April 12. In World War II, the United States liberty ship *SS Adoniram Judson* was named in his honor.

His one surviving son, Edward, spoke at the dedication of the Judson Memorial Church in New York City, summarizing his father's story: "Suffering and success go together. If you are succeeding without suffering, it is because others before you have suffered; if you are suffering without succeeding, it is that others after you may succeed."[14]

---

[14] "Adoniram Judson." Wikipedia. April, 2017.

THE FORGOTTEN BAPTISM

CHAPTER 3

THE VISIONARY PERSON

In 1 Corinthians 10:1-2 we read, "Moreover, brethren, I would not that ye should be ignorant, how that all our fathers were under the cloud, and all passed through the sea; and all were baptized unto Moses in the cloud and in the sea." Paul wanted everyone to know and understand that all our fathers (speaking of Israel) were baptized into Moses.

As mentioned in chapter 1, every baptism has three elements: the baptizer, the person being baptized, and an element into which the baptizer baptizes the person. In water baptism or the baptism of faith, the baptizer, sometimes a minister, will baptize a person into the element of water.

> When it comes to fire baptism, Jesus is the baptizer, the Christian is the person being baptized, and the Holy Spirit is the element into which the baptizer baptizes the person.

When it comes to fire baptism, Jesus is the baptizer, the Christian is the person being baptized, and the Holy Spirit is the element into which the baptizer baptizes the person.

In the verses just mentioned, 1 Corinthians 10:1–2, we find the *forgotten baptism*, the baptism into *servant leadership*.

Moses Leads Us into the Will of God for Our Lives

The Israelites could leave Egypt because of Moses, who was the mediator between the Lord and the Israelites (Gal.

3:19–20). In other words, were it not for Moses, not even one of them would have escaped Egypt. Therefore, their escape is tied to Moses, and accordingly they were associated, or identified, with him. They got out of Egypt because Moses got out of Egypt. Just as we have identified ourselves with Christ in baptism, they identified themselves with Moses when they left Egypt.[15]

To tie the ideas together, the baptism of Moses provides the escape from the slavery of Egypt. In a parallel fashion, the Moses of the New Testament provides escape from the slavery of sin. The escape through the Red Sea is parallel to the resurrection, which is the escape from sin and death by "the Prophet" (Acts 3:19–26), who is the second Moses within the New Testament.

The only difference, however, is that the baptism "into Moses" had to be complemented by the baptism "into the Lord" when they finally entered the Promised Land. That is, when the Israelites entered the Promised Land, it was not Joshua leading the Israelites (successor of Moses), but the Lord himself. The Ark of the Covenant was therefore the agent of baptism into the Promised Land for the Israelites. The Israelites entered the Lord's rest. When their faith was tested in the wilderness, they responded positively.

In summary, in the New Testament, the one who believes in Jesus is akin to the one escaping the power of sin and death (like the Israelites who escaped Egypt). However, subsequent to that time of faith, testing of that faith will ensue in the wilderness of life. If the faith takes root (compare to Matthew 13:1–23), the believer is saved and enters the Promised Land, where more giants await.

Who is Moses? Moses is God's sovereignly ordained leader to lead the people of God into the will of God for their

---

[15] Spencer-Jones, H. D. 1 Corinthians. London; New York: Funk & Wagnalls Company. 1909, p. 322.

lives. When people choose to attend and join a local church, they are not just signing a card and putting their names into a database. In the spirit realm, they are being baptized into "the Moses" of that local church or organization. Who is this Moses? It is God's sovereignly ordained leader, whose assignment is to lead them spiritually into God's will for their lives.

There's an old song in the African-American tradition that asks questions. It says, "Have you been baptized?"

Answer comes back, "Certainly, Lord."

Ask the question again: "Have you been baptized?"

"Certainly, Lord."

"Have you been baptized?"

Answer comes back, "Certainly Lord. Certainly, Lord. Certainly, certainly, certainly Lord."

Have you been baptized into your Moses? Have you recognized that God has sovereignly ordained and ordered your life to bring you to this place, to baptize you into your leader? Your steps have been ordered by God.

People Are in Your Ministry on Purpose

There are probably as many journeys and testimonies in your church or organization as there are people. Everyone has a testimony of where they came from to be baptized into your ministry or organization. They came on purpose. There is not an accident in your ministry. Every person has been sovereignly guided, and their steps were ordered by God to "this place of baptism." God says the spiritual relationship between the pulpit and the pew, between the man of God and the people, is such an intimate spiritual one that it is likened to baptism.

The Bible says they were all baptized into Moses. They were baptized into this visionary, God-ordained leader, this one who would speak the will of God into their lives.[16] Throughout the Body of Christ, people are baptized into visionary leaders because leaders are led by vision. Just as "all of the fathers of Israel" were baptized "into Moses," the Lord desires for the scope of our God-given vision to encompass all the significant leaders in our churches, ministries, or organizations.

It took vision to write this book. It took vision to establish and birth your current church, organization, or ministry. The word root of "video" is *videre*, meaning "to see," and its form *visis* gives us the roots *vid* and *vis*. Words from the Latin *videre* have something to do with "seeing." Vision is the ability "to see." "Vision" comes from the first-person singular form of the Latin root *videre*. It is the Latin word "video," which is transliterated into our culture as "video." Thus, vision is like a video. It is the ongoing scene of the revelation of God's will for your life. Vision is the moving, progressing picture of the ordained will of God.

Vision is the moving, progressing picture of the ordained will of God.

Life Is a Moving Video, Not a Still Snapshot

During our national and international conferences, we normally have photographers take pictures of attendees, speakers, and memorable moments. When the photographer pressed the button on the camera, time was frozen because a snapshot freezes a second or moment in time. Our lives are made up snapshots that are frozen in our minds. Yet God says our lives are to be like a video—a vision that is the ongoing revelation of God's will for our lives.

---

[16] Moffatt 1938: 129; cf. Robertson and Plummer 1914: 200) or "into his leadership" (Calvin 1960: 201; Bruce 1971: 90)

One of the greatest mistakes we could ever make in this life is to assume that life is a snapshot or a series of snapshots that are frozen in our minds. Countless leaders have become stuck in a picture in their past and only see themselves as they were back then instead of the ongoing video revelation of God in their lives.

Ponder some real-life examples with us. Imagine the young man giving his life to Christ in his teenage years. Yet as he matures physically, he stills sees himself as a "babe in Christ" rather than maturing through the ongoing revelation of God in his life. He continues to make immature decisions, decades later, instead of becoming the visionary leader he could have become in this life.

Imagine the founding pastor of a church, taking a mental snapshot of the early days of his church and getting stuck in the past. Years later, he or she continues to talk about the "good ol' days" of the past rather than testifying of the ongoing revelation of God leading him or her through the years.

God's will for your life and ministry is one of a video, not a snapshot. Snapshots are valuable to help you see how far God has brought you, to help you see that you are not where you are going and that you have come farther than where you've been. Snapshots help us measure our lives and give our Lord praise for how far He has brought us. Video, though it consists of individual images, has consistent ongoing movement between each image, moving the viewer forward in time.

The word and concept of "vision" is also related to the word "provide" or "provision." One of the more commonly recognized biblical names of God is Jehovah Jireh. This name of God is revealed in the story of Abraham being called to the mount called Moriah to sacrifice his son, Isaac. When Abraham proves his loyalty and love for God by his willingness to offer his son to the Lord, the angel of God halts the sacrifice. Isaac had prepared the altar and fire for sacrifice and realized that there was no sacrificial lamb. By the way, Isaac was a young man. Some say at least a teenager, while others say he was in his early twenties—not the rosy-cheeked little bouncing baby we often see in the artistic depictions of this scene. Isaac asks his father, "Where is the lamb?"

God Sees Beyond Right Now

It is a question that would echo down the corridors of time and land on the ears of John the Baptist hundreds of years later. While baptizing believers in the Jordan River, John would look up and see one who was as no other man, point to Jesus, and give a prophetic answer to the profound question of Isaac: "Behold the Lamb of God, who takes away the sin of the world" (John 1:29). However, Abraham's answer to his son's sincere query was, "The Lord himself will provide the lamb." The Hebrew phrase for "The Lord will provide" is the name of God, Jehovah Jireh, God is our Provider. The word "provide" means to "pre-see." It comes from the Latin *proōvidēre*, to foresee, or provide for, equivalent to *prō + vidēre*, to see; it means to "pre-see." God is able to *pro-vide* because He is able to *pre-see*!

> We are preoccupied and often so worried and anxious about the problems and challenges we see in the "right now" that our faith is often shaken and our trust in God is weakened.

The problem with flawed finite humanity is our inability to see beyond now. We are so limited in our vision. We are myopic. We are so nearsighted and shortsighted that we cannot see beyond now. We are preoccupied and often so worried and anxious about the problems and challenges we see in the "right now" that our faith is often shaken and our trust in God is weakened. However, God is our provider who has a pro-video, and He is able to pre-see.

So, while we are struggling and wrestling with the problem in the "right now," God is far down the road, and He is seeing in the "not yet." By the time you get from the "right now" to the "not yet," He has moved the problem from the "not yet" into the "no longer," all because He has pre-vision and can pro-vide, and He truly is Jehovah Jireh, our Provider! Your life is not a snapshot, a moment frozen in time. It is a video, an ongoing revelation of God's ordained will for your life. And the camera is still rolling! You are not where you are going. It isn't over until God says it's over. You are where you are, but you are not where you are going. Our God shall supply all your needs because He sees the need before you get there! The camera is still rolling!

How do you see yourself? The mind cannot distinguish between a mental image and an actual image in time. What the mind sees, it believes. If you, for some reason, have gotten stuck in the past image of your life, begin today to reframe that image in your mind by moving toward a video vision of your path from where you were to where you are today. The way you see yourself affects the way others will see you. If you take yourself seriously, others around you will see you "seriously" in their eyes.

In Hebrews 11:22, the Word of God says, "By faith Joseph, when he died, made mention of the departing of the children of Israel; and gave commandment concerning his bones." It was there that God smiled upon Joseph's life because of the faith he demonstrated before the Lord. We believe this story helps us fulfill what the Lord has called us to be, do, and go to in this life. The vision of Joseph's youth came to pass through the corridor of time, regardless of all the obstacles of the pit, prison, and palace.

Remember the Unbreakable Promises of God

As visionary leaders—servant leaders—*we need to remember the unbreakable promises of God*. Hundreds of years earlier, the Lord had given promises to Abraham as it relates to his lineage being given throughout the Earth. He remembers how the Lord spoke to Abraham, Isaac, and Jacob. And the Lord spoke to Joseph, but centuries earlier, when God spoke to Abraham, He shared with him that he was going to have a son, his son was going to become a nation, and that nation would eventually be relocated in a distant land. The people would be forced into slavery, but then there would be an exodus, and the people would come back to the land of Canaan. And God told Abraham it would take at least four hundred years. The Lord was saying to Abraham, in essence, "Abraham, I'm making a promise to you that is larger than you are and longer than your life span. By the time this promise is fulfilled, you will be at peace with your fathers." The God-given vision was beyond the scope of his life on Earth.

Abraham understood what God was up to, so he sought a bride for Isaac. A bride was found, and the process began for the nation of Israel to be born and to be broadened throughout the Earth. We need to remember the unbreakable promises of God. There were times when Joseph was discouraged and, no doubt, from time to time he possibly felt defeated. Yet he did not let the dream die; he did not let the promises be removed from his life. He understood what the promise was, what the plan was. So regardless of the pit, the prison, the palace, or Pharaoh, Joseph was going to be faithful to the assignment. We need to remember the unbreakable promises of God.

You see, some people try to break their promises, and they end up being broken by them. We can either be blessed by God's promises or broken by God's promises, but we'll never bend the promises of God.

Wise is the visionary leader who gets in sync with where God is going and asks God with integrity to bless and to prosper his or her path. Joseph was one of those who understood it in his generation. And even though the promises of God are not given to us, we have inherited them. As Joseph is getting ready to cross the finish line into glory, he pulls his family members together and reminds them of God's promise; he reminds them of where they are headed. And he understands that this message needs to be placed in the hearts of his people.

What's amazing about this story is that 25 percent of the book of Genesis is devoted to this one person named Joseph, yet in the Hall of Fame of Faith, he gets only one verse. That verse is Hebrews 11:22, where Joseph mentions the exodus of the sons of Israel and gives orders concerning his bones. We

> Often people say, "I wish I had enough money." But the question is, do you have enough *vision*? Out of the *vision* comes the *provision*.

want to encourage you to remember the unbreakable promises of God because one day the glory of the Lord will cover the Earth like the water covers the sea. There is not one dry spot on the bottom of the ocean, and one day there will not be a dry spot where the glory of the Lord has not kissed the Earth.

The Bible tells us in Revelation chapter 7 that every tongue, tribe, and nation will stand one day at the throne of God. Now, that is going to happen whether we get involved or not. The Lord will pass us by if we don't get in sync with where He is going. We want to encourage you to remember the unbreakable promises of God. There are more promises than there are problems, and the Holy Trinity never meets in an emergency session. God is not worried about providing for you or for me. Most of the time, we don't have a money problem; we have a vision problem. Often people say, "I wish I had enough money."

But the question is, do you have enough *vision*? Out of the *vision* comes the *provision*.

If you don't have a vision, it doesn't take much money to fund that, but if you have a God-sized vision, you need a God-sized provision to fulfill that. We need to remember the unbreakable promises of God. It's important to understand that when Joseph was in the land of Egypt, he wasn't impressed with the pyramids or by the wealth of the Pharaoh. He understood that God had him on a divine assignment. He saw his role in God's goal. He saw his part in God's heart, and he was faithful to see it through—all the way to placing the vision in the hearts of his children and grandchildren so they could continue the assignment long after he was gone. There are times when problems, stress, and difficulties can discourage any of us, but we need to remember the unbreakable promises of God. We are able to focus on God's promises when we are baptized in leadership.

Realize the Unshakable Power of God

Second, as visionary leaders *we need to realize the unshakable power of God.* You see, companies begin, and companies close; denominations start, and they stop; and empires are raised up, and they come crashing down. Yet the Kingdom of God has never experienced a recession. The Kingdom of God continues to grow every year. The church is growing faster today than it has ever grown before. We are living in the greatest times of evangelism, church planting, global networking, and the possibility of fulfilling the Great Commission in this century. And we need to realize the unshakable power of God.

We want you to see what Joseph chose to do. Joseph pulled his family members together. No doubt there were concerns all around him, and there are concerns all around you. Joseph understood that life was about to change for him and for those following behind him. But how did Joseph handle it? When he pulled his family members together, did he fill them with worry and anxiety, dread and doubt? No. He reminded them of God's plan; he reminded them of the mission. He reminded them of where they were headed. By the way, the next time the devil reminds you of your past, just remind him of his destined future. Joseph realized the unshakable power of God. He knew that God was going to see it through to the end. In fact, Joseph had demonstrated this confidence years earlier when his father had passed away.

When Joseph's father, Jacob, had passed away, as you may recall, Joseph stopped what he was doing, and he took his dad back to the land of promise to a small village called Shechem. *Shechem* means a place of prosperity. He took his dad back to prosperity, buried him there, returned, and stayed on the assignment. See, he realized where his home would be. He understood where the people were going, and he made a deposit by burying his dad in the land of promise. In doing so, he pulled his family members together. He didn't fill them with worry, doubt, and dread; he renewed them, encouraged them, and let them know everything was going to be great and wonderful down the road.

Would there be labor instead of favor? Would there be famine instead of feasting? Yes. Would there be hardship and headache and heartache? Yes. But God would see them through to the other side. Frankly, it doesn't matter who the pharaoh is, and it doesn't matter how many chariots you may have. When God says He's going to do something, you can count on it. He's going to do it.

No doubt there were concerns all around him. No doubt there are concerns all around you. No doubt there are financial and family concerns. No doubt there are health and ministerial concerns. No doubt there are many different obstacles that you may be facing as you read this. However, the Lord, who started you on the journey, wants to help you finish what you started. He wants to give you enough money, enough momentum, and enough people in your life so that you will be able to achieve great things by working together.

Not only were there concerns all around Joseph; there was change. Real, dramatic change was coming. And radical change has impacted your life and mine. This generation, specifically in the past ten to fifteen years, has experienced more change than any other generation since the beginning of time. In the past twenty to thirty years, more dramatic informational and technological change has happened on the planet that has catapulted the nations of the Earth forward in a way that no other previous generation has ever experienced. Yet we're not fearful of the change; we welcome it.

Joseph knew that change was coming for him. He knew he was passing away and that his time on Earth was going to be over. What he had to do, he had to do decisively and quickly to make sure that his family members were ready to continue what he had started. Often, people talk about their legacy, what they're leaving behind. Often, we reflect on not just what we're leaving behind but on what we've started while here on the Earth. Our prayer is that we start more ripples than we will ever be able to see completed in our short tenure in the world.

There were no doubt concerns around Joseph and change around him and before him, and no doubt there is change coming for you; there's change coming for us. But it's important to understand the chronology that is behind us. We have come a long way in a short period of time.

It's also important for us to understand that Joseph understood the chronology behind him. He knew that the day was coming when God was going to fulfill the promise of the exodus from the world. The Prophet Habakkuk exhorts us to write the vision down—write it down in plain and concise language so that we might run with it. The vision that God has put in your heart needs to be clear and concise so that you might run with it. We need to understand that the history behind us is prologue, and our future is bright and brilliant before us. And we need to realize the unshakable power of God. It doesn't really matter what the armies of the Earth may say or do, and it doesn't really matter what empires are raised up in the years ahead. God is going to keep His word, and God is going to use people who want to be used. God is in the extra that turns the ordinary into the extraordinary. God is our extra. It's

"Let my people go."

the extra things He does for us every day. It's the extra people He sends along our path. It's the extra thoughts He puts in our hearts. It's the extra faith He puts in our lives. It's the extra abilities He gives to us so we can do the extraordinary and we can be about the Lord's business and believe it is possible to fulfill the Great Commission in our generation.

Rest in the Unmistakable Peace of God

Third, as visionary leaders, *we need to rest in the unmistakable peace of God.* Sometimes we wonder, "Is the Lord going to come through? Is the Lord going to be on time?" The Lord is never late, and He always does come through with His plan for His person.

When we think of Joseph as he crosses the finish line, he smiles at death. I'm sure you don't have anything worse than death stalking you; we know we certainly don't have anything worse than death stalking us. And as Joseph crosses death, he smiles at it, and his family members lay him to rest. One year goes by, five years go by, a hundred years go by. One day, Moses walks into Pharaoh's court and demands, "Let my people go." This is the day of divine exodus. This is one of the big red-letter days on God's calendar. And it's on this day that Moses, the great general, leads nearly two million people out of Egypt. This is the phenomenal exodus that God had spoken to Abraham about centuries earlier. This is the day that God said His people were going to leave the nation of Egypt.

As Moses gathers the people, they make their way out of Egypt. They haven't traveled very far when the Bible tells us in the Exodus, 13:17–19 that Moses gives the command to go find the body of Joseph. He gives a command, in fact, concerning the bones of Joseph. Don't think for one skinny second that Moses and the people left Joseph behind. I was taught in Sunday School that two people went into Canaan, but as you're going to see, three people went into Canaan who originally began in Egypt. Joseph came out, and Joseph went in.

It's at this point in time that they get the box that contains the bones of Joseph and bring Joseph out of Egypt. The Bible doesn't tell us how this all happened, but as you will see in a few moments, it did take place. As they bring Joseph out of Egypt, we believe they took him to the front of the line. Of course the Bible doesn't tell us where they positioned Joseph on this trip out of Egypt, but we have a hard time believing they brought him out and put him at the back of two million people. We believe they brought him to where Moses was and began to carry Joseph. How long did they carry him? They carried him the entire time of their wilderness wanderings—that's forty years. They carried him through the Red Sea, they carried him by Mount Sinai, and they carried him by Mount Nebo where God buried Moses. But Joseph didn't stop there; he continued right on.

In fact, what's so amazing is that every day, no doubt, in the land of the wilderness they buried Israelites; they buried an entire generation of Israelites. And God raised up an entire generation that would go into the land of Canaan. Every day somebody died. But Joseph wasn't buried in the land of wilderness wanderings; he was taken all the way to Canaan. There was more faith in the bones of Joseph than there was in the feet of the Israelites. Joseph went right through the Red Sea, and he went by Gilgal and Jericho, and he was there the day the sun stood still. You may ask, "How do you know that?"

The Bible tells us so. The Word of God tells us in Joshua 24, the very last paragraph, beginning in verse 22, that it was there that they buried Joseph in Shekem. Now, *Shekem* is a familiar word; it was there that Joseph had buried Jacob more than a hundred years earlier, when he was the prime minister of Egypt. It was at the end of the battles that they took the body of Joseph and buried him next to his dad, Jacob, in Shekem, a place of prosperity.

Think about this amazing story for a moment. Here is Joseph, who is sold into slavery, falsely accused, and put into prison. He is then brought to the palace and made the second in command, and he is buried in Egypt.

What God begins, He finishes.

They carry him through the wilderness wanderings, through the years in Canaan, through all the battles, and now they bury him next to his dad, Jacob, more than a hundred years later. What God begins, He finishes. We need to remember the unbreakable promises of God, we need to realize the unshakeable power of God, and we need to rest in the unmistakable peace of God.

When you think about it, there are many change agents who come and go in this world, but there are only a few who can say at the end of life's journey, "Not only did I help to bring change, but I helped to bring salvation."

As we come to the end of this chapter, there's one perplexing question we want to ask you: Why was Joseph discontent about being left in Egypt? Why didn't he encourage his family to go on to the land of Canaan, and one day they would all rendezvous in glory? Why was he so emphatic in saying, "When God takes you out, you must take me with you"? I believe the answer is simply this: Joseph wanted to be involved in what God was doing, whether he was dead or alive. He had a driving desire to be included in God's plan in establishing the Kingdom on the Earth. We believe that if you will cultivate, as a visionary leader, that kind of passion, your reservoir will never run dry, and your fountainhead will never be dammed up. You will never burn out; neither will you rust out!

We challenge you to become a visionary leader in this generation and mobilize your church, ministry, or organization to be baptized into the God-sized vision that has been entrusted to you.

Visionary Leader Spotlight: William Cameron Townsend

"The greatest missionary is the Bible in the mother tongue. It needs no furlough and is never considered a foreigner."

Those words became the motto of the man behind Wycliffe Bible Translators, without a doubt the twentieth century's greatest Bible-translating organization. William Cameron Townsend, like James Hudson Taylor I, is often not known by his first name. He became "Cameron" to many and simply "Cam" to others.

Both his general and spiritual education began in his hometown of Downey, California. As a teenager, he joined the Presbyterian church that his family attended.

To further his education, Cameron entered the Presbyterian-owned Occidental College in Los Angeles. In his junior year, he heard guest speaker John Mott of the Student Volunteer Movement. Mott challenged students to commit their lives to missionary service. His passion captured

Cameron's attention. He personally met with John and signed up to go to those who had never heard the Gospel.

At that time, America's involvement in World War I seemed inevitable. Cameron enlisted in the National Guard. When America entered the war, a missionary pressed upon him to seek a deferment so he could instead serve God in the fight for souls. His captain accepted Cam's request, telling him, "Go. You'll do a lot more good selling Bibles in Central America than you would shooting Germans in France." So instead of Europe, Cameron headed for Latin America to hold services and sell Bibles in Guatemala.

His breakthrough came toward the end of his first year in the villages of the Cakchiquel Indians. One day, Cameron walked into a beer garden to distribute the Gospel. He offered a tract to a native sitting at one of the tables, drinking. The man said, "Sorry, señor, but I cannot read." However, when Cameron left, the man followed him, saying, "Amigo, I have a friend who reads. Will you sell me the little book, por favor?" Cameron gave the native the tract and invited him to a Sunday service. The man showed up and responded at the close of the service to become a Christian.[17]

Nearly a year of traveling through other Latin American countries increased Cam's desire to take the Gospel to that part of the world. The extended assignment led to another aspect of his future: he met a young female missionary who felt the same call. Cameron and Elvira married in July 1919. Together, they started a mission school.

Cameron wanted to create a written language for the Cakchiquel Indians. He developed a method for gradually introducing the language in written form, writing primers to aid both children and adult students. His biggest dream (up to that point) was to translate the entire New Testament into

---

[17] Bruce Smith, Wycliffe Associates; Interview with James O. Davis, Cutting Edge International, November, 2016.

the Cakchiquel language. Cameron tackled his vision with fervor. However, there were delays. Among other setbacks, Cameron contracted tuberculosis. He returned to California to recover, eventually completing the Bible in 1929, after ten full years.

Cameron's dream expanded. Why shouldn't other tribes without written languages have translations in their native tongue? So in 1934, he initiated the Summer Institute of Linguistics (SIL) on a farm in Arkansas to train workers to translate. SIL grew year after year.

He named the location Camp Wycliffe, after John Wycliffe, the fourteenth-century translator of the English Bible. In 1942, Cameron incorporated his missionary work as Wycliffe Bible Translators.

Lazaro Cardenas, the president of Mexico, invited Cameron in 1936 to bring a team to help those of his country who had no written language. Cam agreed.

After World War II, the ministry grew even further. One boost in interest and support came in 1956 after the violent deaths of SIL graduate Jim Elliot and his fellow martyrs. Their deaths at the hands of the Ecuadorian Indians that they were trying to help inspired others to willingly commit to the cause of spreading the gospel to those who had never heard it.

In 1942, the year Cameron incorporated Wycliffe Bible Translators, American universities began requesting classes teaching the SIL linguistics method. The following year Elvira died, adding sorrow to the joy of those years of progress and expansion. Cameron formed the final arm of his ministry in 1948: Jungle Aviation and Radio Service. He started JAARS to pilot and keep in contact with missionaries in the jungle.

During the 1960s, Wycliffe gained a presence in Africa and Asia.

When Cameron died from leukemia on April 23, 1982, he'd given more than sixty years of his life to helping groups of people around the world receive God's Word in their native languages. By the year 2000, Wycliffe Bible Translators had made the New Testament accessible in nearly five hundred languages. Today, Wycliffe Bible Translators are moving faster than ever before, providing hundreds of new language translations per year. It is estimated that by 2025, the beginnings of a Bible will have the beginnings of being translated into every known language![18]

---

[18] Bruce Smith, Wycliffe Associates; Interview with James O. Davis, Cutting Edge International, November, 2016.

CHAPTER 4

THE VISIONARY PROCESS

God is the author of vision. His nature is to be providential and purposeful. With this in mind, we are thinking about a specific kind of vision in the church, organization, or ministry. God appointed the Earth to be both the scene of the revelation of His invisible essence and for the operation of His eternal vision, for His created masterpiece.

God had vision for man, as described in Genesis 1:26–28. God prepared the Earth. God created man with a purpose. Man was to multiply. In Psalm 8:1–4, the psalmist writes about how excellent God's vision was in the Earth. God's vision was so high above the heavens and the Earth, people could hardly understand how great man was to be. God simply thought it, and it was so.

Enlightenment of Vision Inside the Leader

Creation was brought into reality from nothing but God's Word. Creation progressed from a state of nothingness through a state of formlessness and emptiness to a condition when formlessness gave way to form and emptiness surrendered to fullness. This explains the creation of vision by God. Vision is also created in leaders who carry vision. Visionary leaders progress from a state of nothingness to a state of formlessness.

As we start to envision everything about the Kingdom of God, there's no form, no fullness, and no fruit yet. This is why you are a visionary leader. You can actually see ahead of time where barrenness can break forth and be fruitful. You can actually see where nothing will become something.

A leader, or "bishop," is an *episkopos* in Greek. *Episkopos* has been translated as "overseer" for decades in Greek commentaries. The word *episkopos* consists of the words *epi* and *skopos*. *Epi* is "to look beyond," and *skopos* is "to focus." Thus, when we talk about *episkopos*, it means "the ability to see over something and beyond something." [19]

Actually, *episkopos* was not pastoral in nature; it was prophetic in nature. The term dealt with vision and can refer to a leader who has a great pastoral heart. Yet if you only have a pastoral heart, it would be very hard for you to lead a congregation into a God-sized vision because you have to have an *episkopos*

> Visionary leaders progress from a state of nothingness to a state of formlessness.

as well. You have to see further than other people. You have to be able to see over the obstacles. You have to be able to see that where there is nothing, there's going to be something. You have to be able to see where something is empty, but it's going to be full.

Other people can't see it, and they might even question what you see, but that is "the God" piece in leadership that makes you a visionary leader. This is the power of vision at work, the power of leadership baptism. Vision turns nothingness and emptiness into something and fulfillment. Genesis 1:1–2 says, "In the beginning God created heaven and the earth. And the earth was without form, and void;

---

[19] "Presbyter." Wikipedia. May 21, 2017.

And darkness was upon the face of the deep..." Scripture says the Spirit of God hovered over all that, and then something began to happen.

Execution of the Vision through the Leader

As a leader, one of the most important things you will ever do is see and lead with vision. Yes, you may be a pastor.

> This is the power of vision at work, the power of leadership baptism. Vision turns nothingness and emptiness into something and fulfillment.

All leaders should shepherd the people of God and have a pastoral spirit, but it takes certain leaders to be "seers." In the Old Testament, the prophets were called "seers." Why?

They could see things other people couldn't see. They saw things hundreds or thousands of years in the future. As a leader, you are supposed to be able to see things as you move the organization into the future.[20]

God is the initiator, and the leader responds to and implements the vision. God initiates the vision Himself. You, as the leader, respond to God's initiation—that is, you understand God's purpose from Scripture. And then you, as a visionary leader, are responsible for implementing the vision wherever you live, in whatever nation, society, culture, city, and town you are in. You're responsible for implementing the vision that God has already given, not the one you dreamed up.

It's not just what you want to do; it's what God wants to do. It is what God has said He's going to do. When you become a part of God's vison, you are beginning to have a thorough understanding of what the church is, where the

---

[20] Damazio, Frank. Synergize 2012 Pastors And Leaders Conference. 2012. Orlando, Florida.

church is going, and how to lead others into the baptism of the vision. You now have a thorough understanding of what the Kingdom of God is and of the nature and work of the Holy Spirit. As a visionary leader, you will have to have more than the latest business books to implement the vision God has given to you. As indicated in chapters 1 and 2, you will need faith and fire to sustain and strengthen you throughout the visionary journey.

God is the source of vision, revealed in His vision of those people who have hearts to receive it and minds to understand it. In Hebrews 1:1, there are many revelations, each of which is portion of the truth. In many different ways, God spoke to our fathers in and by the prophets.

Explanation of the Vision for the Leader

In Isaiah 28:10, we learn of "precept upon precept" and "line upon line." This is how vision works when it comes forth from God. It doesn't usually come all at the same time; rather, it comes line upon line until we begin to see what God sees and we apply it to our world. The biblical fact that we are created in the image of God means our basic function is to reflect God. As human beings, we have the potential to see into the future, to have vision for what is possible, and to move toward that vision.

As a born-again person, you have the Holy Spirit, and because you have the Holy Spirit, you have the potential to be like God. To be like God means you have to have vision. You cannot be a Spirit-filled leader, and not be a person of vision. You must have capacity for faith, the capacity to build, and the capacity to see where formlessness will give way to a form because of the Holy Spirit working in your life. You have to have the capacity to see what is barren but is going to become fruitful. This is the essence of what we're talking about here—the ability to see those things that are not as they were.

That's what the Bible says about Abraham, a man of faith. He saw things other people couldn't see. Actually, they didn't exist yet, but he could see that they "are not" as they were. They already existed in his faith realm. This is what a visionary leader is.

Moses was challenged to "see the salvation of the Lord" while standing at the edge of the Red Sea. The Lord was allowing him to see first before he stood on dry ground. The visionary leader sees first, sees the farthest, and sees the longest.

Understanding vision requires a view from above. When you have vision or become a visionary leader, you understand what vision is. You see things from a different angle, and that view is from above. Vision is having the ability to see into the future. The future doesn't seek to replicate the past; it seeks to create something new.

> **The future doesn't seek to replicate the past; it seeks to create something new.**

To become a visionary leader is not just to copy the past or copy what others have done. It is to create something new and possibly something nobody has done yet. When we become visionary leaders, we enter a powerful adventure. This is where leaders will gain the ability to have fervor and passion because they're seeing things no one else is seeing, and they want to be involved with fulfilling God's vision. This is part of God's will for your life.

Examples of Vision with the Leader

Vision starts with an encounter with God. In 2 Chronicles 1:7–12, God appeared to Solomon and encouraged him to ask of God what he wanted. Four times in the Bible, the phrase "Ask whatever you want and I will give it to you."

Solomon told God, in essence, "You've shown me great mercy, and Lord, I know I'm king, but this is what I'm going to ask for." He asked for a specific thing, and God said to him, basically, "I'm going to give you this. I'm going to give you wisdom and knowledge to shepherd my people. I'm also going to give you what you didn't ask for because you asked for the right thing out of the right motive. I'm going to give you riches, wealth, and honor. I'm going to give you promotion, prestige, and a legacy."

Solomon had such a wonderful vision that he began with—the vision of God. If he had stayed with the same heart throughout his journey, he would have had the same things God told him he would have. Sometimes, because God is so good, vision can ruin a leader's heart, if his or her heart is not filled with integrity to carry the blessing and favor of God.

Why doesn't God show so much blessing and favor to everybody? It's because some people can't handle it. God knows the vision will destroy them. God knows He will set them up for failure. He knows that they were never prepared properly. Their hearts cannot handle promotion and favor. God sometimes withholds the good things because our hearts are not ready to grasp all the good things.

We should spend most of our lives preparing our hearts and our character because the vision God wants to reveal is so far above anything we could imagine. The God-given vision will come, but we must have the heart and character to handle it. When vision comes, it comes through the grid, or through the filters of our own lives. Vision comes through the filter of your past, how you see things, your worldview.

Wherever you are in the world, when vision comes to you, you have to take the vision through your grid, through your filters, through your culture, education, background, through your mind, will, emotions, insight, and through your spiritual maturity, and out comes the vision that makes it through all your filters.

The visionary leader should have a personal vision and an organizational vision that lays out a course to follow that makes vision a reality. Every leader needs to have a personal vision for his or her life, ministry, and calling. Leadership baptism impacts all aspects of our lives.

You also must have a corporate vision—a vision for the church Jesus is building and the purpose of that church. The two visions must work together. The receiving of vision will bring motivation and passion, direction, purpose, and strategy. Responding to the vision will bring clarity about what you should be building.

Noah received the vision to build what had never before existed—the ark. We want God to give you a Noah-type encounter in which you see something that has never been seen before and build something that has never existed before.

Noah was like Abraham and Moses. He had a vision of receiving the sevenfold blessings of God. Noah received a vision of something that had never been built. Abraham receive a

> **Noah received the vision to build what had never before existed–the ark.**

blessing that no one had ever received before. Because of the vision that came to him in Genesis chapter 12, the dream so overtook him that he had to walk in faith.

Why is Abraham called "the father of faith"? Because the vision he received was beyond human strength and human intensity. It had spiritual intensity, and he believed in something no one else would hope for—the full blessings of God.

Joseph had a vision of unmistakable supremacy that would happen through his own lineage and life. Furthermore, Joseph saw that the Kingdom of God would be supreme and that God himself would rule through him in a situation that would be far too hard for one individual to ever make happen. Joseph's whole life is a testimony of the sovereignty and grace of God. His vision, as you might remember, was something that would cause the Word of God to rule and reign supremely in his generation.

Moses had a vision of changing the course of history. It cost him forty years in the wilderness. Joshua had a vision of leading the next generation. He had no idea what he was doing when he said he would lead that generation because the people of that generation were hard-hearted, stiff-necked, and rebellious. Moses was literally destroyed by that generation in his own ministry. Then Joshua encountered that same group of people, and they came together to follow his leadership. He was willing to take the next generation and lead them into something new that only God could put in front of them.

The apostle Paul had a vision of building world-changing churches. He planted more churches and trained more leaders and pastors in his time than anybody else. His vision was to plant thriving churches worldwide.

Examinations of Vision for the Leader

As a visionary leader, what do you see? What is in your heart? What vision do you have? The vision of seeing beyond and over everything? What are the obstacles right now that would stop you from building a thriving church in your town, your village, your area, your city, or your nation or from multiplying those churches into dozens and then hundreds? Is the obstacle that you don't have enough leaders to do that? Then create a pipeline. Create a strategy. Believe God can and will do that because God can help you have leaders. Is the obstacle one of finances? Resources? Do you think you just don't have the means to make that large of a vision come to pass?

Whatever the obstacle is, whether it's resources or people, or you don't have the land and property for the vision and the building, we want you to know right now that God is able to provide whatever you need if the vision is the Lord's. If it's the Lord's will, the vision will come to pass.

There are at least four summary principles for visionary leadership:

1. The principle of *possessing the vision*. You receive the God-sized vision in prayer, an encounter, through the Holy Spirit. In Habakkuk 2:1 (we will come back to Habakkuk a little later), we read, "I will stand my watch, set myself on the rampart, and I will watch to see what

> Find people who will stand with you and say, "You know, this is the vision of God."

he will say to me and what I will answer when I hear it." Now, you need to set yourself aside, and you need to pray, fast, and call on the name of the Lord.

2. The principle of *processing the vision*. You have to have some implementation principles that guide you in knowing how to process this. Hear it. Write it down. Get counseled.

3. The principle of *passing on the vision*. Find people to whom you can impart the vision. Find people who have the same spirit and faith you have. Find people who will stand with you and say, "You know, this is the vision of God."

4. The principle of *pacing the vision*. You need to know how fast you can do it and how slow you have to go at times. You will have to pace it through people. If

59

you learn to pace the vision right, then all the leaders can join with you and fulfill that vision.[21]

For a visionary leader to be a phenomenal leader, he or she must not only receive the vision personally; that leader also must impart the vision to everybody around him or her, making sure all the people are on the same page, walking on the same path, embracing the same values, and proceeding in unity of mind. This truth is as important as hearing from God; as important as people who would have to set themselves up to know God and pass it on. If the visionary leader is not able to pass it on and pace it through others, then very few followers will be baptized into the vision.

Develop Your Capacity for Vision

The leader's development of vision capacity is critical to the success of the vision. Capacity is competency, fitness, and suitability for accommodating the maximum amount that can be contained. Capacity is the decision to be

> If you don't want to change, the vision will be quenched by your own lack of flexibility, the limits of your inner world.

enlarged so you can hold on to all that God desires to pour in—limited only by God's largeness in giving, not by our smallness to contain. Vision capacity is connected to you as an individual and is affected by your level of character, faith, and spiritual hunger.

We need to remember that our level of character, faith, and hunger have a lot to do with the size of vision God will give

[21] Damazio, Frank. Synergize 2012 Pastors And Leaders Conference. 2012. Orlando, Florida.

us. You must be willing to change because sometimes God will give you a vision that will stretch your wineskin. If you don't want to change, the vision will be quenched by your own lack of flexibility, the limits of your inner world.

If you've received vision but you're spiritually not able to take the vision forward, the vision will die inside of you because your inner world, your inner man or woman, and your heart can't carry it. The womb of vision is the heart. The level of mental discipline, emotional health, resilience, knowledge, and passion all have something to do with how you will handle the vision.

You must bring ownership to your teams and to every leader you work with regarding how they will own the vision. You cannot lead a great church or organization if the leaders don't own the vision. This means they have to be birthed into it, and they have to understand it. You have to take time with them, pray with them, and impart it deeply into their hearts.

Owning the vision means this: as a leader, I commit myself to understanding the vision and values of our church, organization, or ministry. I will personally assimilate the vision into my spirit, soul, and mind. I will make the vision my vision, and I will commit my heart to have faith for the vision and impart it to others. That's what it means to own the vision.

Now, if every visionary leader had that kind of a heart, we would have a world-class team. Everybody would be owning the vision, carrying the vision, and passing it on. The leader must first be baptized into the God-sized vision that God has given. Then he or she will have the opportunity to move the whole church or organization into the prosperous aspects of this vision.[22]

The leader fulfills the vision by being aligned with the Lord and the vision. Unaligned leaders in any realm of leadership,

---

[22] Damazio, Frank. Synergize 2012 Pastors And Leaders Conference. 2012. Orlando, Florida.

61

any place of the church or organization, are in danger of causing the ministry to limp into the vision instead of running with it.

Unaligned leaders are leaders who form subcultures and create sub-visions, or smaller visions, within the vision that has already been given by the local church. Visionary leaders who are in alignment with the ministry they lead when they're in alignment with the vision see the big picture and fulfill the big picture. We should get rooted in that kind of vision and train leaders this way in the future.

Visionary Leader Spotlight: Sir Edmund Hillary

Sir Edmund Hillary is generally considered to be the last great visionary explorer of the twentieth century. He was the one who first reached the summit of Mt. Everest, the first one to cross Antarctica and the South Pole, and the first one to reach the North Pole.

Sir Edmund Hillary climbed Mt. Everest in 1953. One author wrote about how Sir Edmund tried to reach the summit in 1952 but failed to conquer the mountain. Many trained climbers had

> Half the battle is getting up; the other half is getting back down.

tried to make it up the mountain and failed. Even if they got partway up, they failed on the descent.

When Sir Edmund trekked back down in defeat, some laughed at him, and others openly mocked him. Who was he, trying to do what no one had ever done? He was just an ordinary beekeeper!

At a press conference held in Auckland, New Zealand, for Sir Edmund about his experience, he surprised everyone. He hung a large picture of Everest on the wall behind him. Some of the reporters took the opportunity to remind him, "It's not possible to climb Mt. Everest. Even if you could get to the top, you could not live there. You would surely die on the top or die on your way back down. Half the battle is getting up; the other half is getting back down."

The young Edmund Hillary stood in front of that audience and said, "Look at the picture of Mt. Everest behind me."

Then he said, "I want you to see how large it is. I want you to see how wide it is. Mt. Everest stopped growing a long time ago, but Edmund Hillary hasn't stopped growing yet. A year from today, I will climb to the top of Mt. Everest. I will hoist high the British flag, and I will stand where no one has ever stood before."

A year later, on May 29, 1953, Edmund Hillary did it. He stood on what he aptly called the "Roof of the World."

As leaders, with many decisions ahead of us, we need to realize that a vision becomes a goal only when we put a date with it. Edmund Hillary could have said, "Someday I'm going to climb to the top. Someday I'll go and stand where no one has stood. Someday I think I'll try to do this." Instead he was very specific and very strategic. He declared, "A year from today, I will climb to the top of Mt. Everest, I will hoist high the British Flag and I will stand where no one has ever stood before."

Sir Edmund made a profound statement: *"The mountain has stopped growing, but I am still growing!"*

Even with his fame, Sir Edmund was a very giving and gracious man. He helped raise money from around the world for the people who lived in the Himalayan Mountains. He was known for the twenty-seven schools he started and the airports he founded in that region of the world.

In August 2007, I (James Davis) was thinking once more about Sir Edmund. I was facing some difficult circumstances in my life, but I knew, without a doubt, that I could climb the mountain standing in my path. I decided to take action after all those years and sent an e-mail to Auckland, New Zealand, to an office worker I found who I believed could assist me. I wrote, "If I could have fifteen minutes with Sir Edmund Hillary, I'll get on a plane and fly to Auckland, New Zealand. When the fifteen minutes are up, I will return to the United States of America."

A few days went by, and the office worker wrote to give me several different dates that I could consider visiting with Sir Edmund Hillary in his home. I chose August 31, 2007.

If you had pulled up into Sir Edmund Hillary's driveway, you would not have known from the outside of that humble home that living behind those walls was one of the great explorers of all time. You would not have guessed that Sir Edmund Hillary and his sweet wife, Lady June, lived there. When we met them, we immediately saw that Sir Edmund was just as unassuming as his house. He was very down-to-earth, humble, and a gracious gentleman. He and his wife welcomed us into their home with generous hospitality. It was a warm welcome—a joy and a delight. Most importantly, I received some of the greatest wisdom that I have ever personally received in those two hours.

At some point, each visionary leader has to make a decision about what size of life he or she will live in our shrinking world. We are each required to decide whether we will live a life beyond the parameters of everyday existence, a life that pursues the largeness of spirit that we see in the life of Sir Edmund Hillary, or if we'll live only to ourselves and our private ambitions.

The first question I asked Sir Edmund was simply this: "How do I become a focused person?" I said to him, "There are many adventures in life. There are many things I could be about, many things I can do or try, but how can I become really focused?"

Sir Edmund sat very quietly for a moment. When we met, he was eighty-eight years old. Although he had scaled the heights of his profession, and had experienced much fame and success, he had known his share of sadness as well. He had buried his first wife and their daughter. While watching a plane take off carrying his wife and daughter, for the maiden voyage, from an airport in the Himalayan Mountain Region he had raised funds to build, the plane crashed at the end of the runway. The pain must have been unbearable. We didn't talk much about those things when we were together. He had lived an enormous life in spite of tragedies he had faced.

Sir Edmund just sat quietly. It appeared that perhaps he had not heard the question. I sat there wondering if I should repeat myself or just let the great man form his answer.

I was happy that I decided to wait for his response. What he said became indelibly imprinted on my mind the moment the words were out of his mouth. Sir Edmund said, "If you only do what others have already done, then you will only feel what others have already felt. But if you would dare to do something that no one else has ever done, then you'll have a satisfaction that no one else has ever felt."

As you ponder these words, they become even more powerful and profound. In every visionary leader's life, there is the need for focus and the desire for vision. With vision comes focus. With focus comes exactitude. Exactitude creates priorities for each and every day. Being baptized in leadership infuses us with an unquenchable desire to pave the pathway for those we lead to discover God's will.

The lack of real, focused vision encourages people to chase aimlessly after *everything*, trying for the rest of their lives to find that hidden treasure. Once leaders have chosen what unique path is theirs and know it is a God-given, divinely ordained path, they don't chase endlessly after doors of opportunities. They know the path that they are to walk.

Edmund Hillary added another sentence after his initial response to the question. He said, "When you're choosing your life's project, if there's no fear involved, then you will become bored with it, and you won't even finish what you have begun."

We wonder if we sometimes choose molehills instead of mountaintops because we don't want the fear of scaling something bigger to gnaw and nag at our lives. As a result, we choose a subpar life rather than a greater God-filled life.

As leaders, it is okay to set personal goals and try to achieve them. There's nothing wrong with setting personal goals and nothing wrong with trying to achieve them. Yet the roles and goals that God has for us are bigger than our own roles and goals. His goal is that every person on the planet hear the glorious Gospel of Jesus Christ. The Christian's greatest Mount Everest is putting the cross of Jesus Christ on the roof of the world.[23]

> There's nothing wrong with setting personal goals and nothing wrong with trying to achieve them.

---

[23] Davis, James O. *Scaling Your Everest: Lessons Learned From Sir Edmund Hillary.* Billion Soul Publishers, 2014.

CHAPTER 5

THE VISIONARY PROBLEMS

Visionary leaders lead through vision, bringing people from an undesirable past to a preferable future. However, from time to time, there can be problems with the video or the ongoing revelation of God in our lives.

A while back, my wife and I (Kenneth Ulmer) were watching a movie. We had satellite TV, and as we watched the movie, an unusually severe southern California storm arose. The wind was howling, and rain was beating against our windows while we were engrossed in the story line of the movie, which was getting more and more intriguing. All of a sudden, the screen went black! We sat looking at each other, not only wondering what happened, but frustrated because we were missing a good part of the movie!

Soon after that, the screen went white with a hissing sound, and snow covered the screen! Now we were more confused because we didn't know if the storm had blown away the satellite dish or if there was some electrical problem in the house. As we sat there wondering what, if anything, could we do, a sign came up on the black screen: "Searching for Signal." Searching for signal—that is part of the reality of the video of vision. Searching for signal—that is often an accurate description of scenes in vision revelation.

This is a season of the visionary video that every leader knows at some point in his or her life. Every leader knows of those dark nights when your soul and your heart is searching for a signal. "What's next, God? Where did this come from, God? That's not what I remember seeing, God. In fact, Lord, I can't see." The blackness of indecision. The snow of confusion. The hissing sound of the discouraging taunts of the enemy. "Oh, God, my soul, my heart, my mind—I'm searching for a signal." Leadership baptism provides you with an inner compass of sorts, a signal that points you in the right direction.

Leaders Sometimes Search for Signals from God

God brought hundreds or even thousands of people to your ministry, organization, or church in a signal-searching season, when your heart and your mind and your life are experiencing the snow of confusion. Or maybe God has not brought the masses to your place of ministry. You know what it's like to

> "Oh, God, my soul, my heart, my mind—I'm searching for a signal."

stand outside the almost empty church looking longingly to the heavens as your soul searches for a signal. "What am I doing wrong? Where did I get off course? Where did I make a wrong turn?" Searching for a signal. In the snow of confusion, it seems you are trying to help people who don't want to be helped, save people who don't want to be saved, and speak to those who don't want to hear. And your soul is searching for a signal!

"Lord, what next? Where do I go next?" It's one thing to be lost and not know where you are or where you are going; it's quite another thing to be lost and look behind you to see that people are following you. They are looking to you, asking, "What next?" And you are looking to God with the same question: "Lord, what next? My soul is searching for a signal." God brought you this far, and you are now searching for a signal because of the unexpected disconnect of leadership with God. There are those times when we're trying to lead the people, and we don't have a spiritual signal or divine connection. "What's next? What's the next chapter? Where do we go from here? How did we get here? How do we move on from here?"

In the midst of the storm in your soul, you're searching for a signal. This problematic situation raises an interesting question: What do you do, and what do the people do, in those seasons when you are searching? In other words, the people are following the leader, and the leader doesn't know what's next. People are following the visionary, and the visionary has lost the vision. At this point in time, another very logical question arises: Why follow someone in those seasons when they themselves are searching? It's a legitimate question. If, in fact, the visionary, the leader, the pastor, the Moses, has seasons of searching, why follow someone when they're not always sure where they're going? If you don't know where you're going, why would—why should—they follow you?

In 1 Samuel 14 is a scene in which Jonathan is leading one man, his armor bearer, into a camp against the enemy. Jonathan says, "I have a vision. The vision is, let's go and take this camp." The armor bearer does a head count and realizes there are only two of them. One more time Jonathan says, basically, "I have a vision. The vision is, let's go, just the two of us, into this camp and take this thing for God. We can take this! We can do this! The God we serve is such a God. He can get victory by many, or He can get victory through the two of us."

Now, if I were an armor bearer for Jonathan, I would say, "Excuse me. Excuse me. Excuse me. Let me understand this. Your vision is that just the two of us could take this camp? Can you see very well? Are you seeing? Have you done a count of this opposition that we have?"

I used to think that the most important thing was that the people who follow you catch your vision. I used to believe that the most important thing was that you share your vision with them. The priority of leadership is vision. Vision, vision, vision. But what about those times when the vision makes no sense? What about those times when you can't see the vision yourself, and you're supposed to be the leader? Your vision is cloudy, and it makes no sense. Why would people follow you? Jonathan had a nonsensical vision. It made no sense, why would the armor bearer follow him?

In 1 Samuel 14:7, the armor bearer said, "Do all that is in thine heart: turn thee; behold, I am with thee according to thy heart." What is the armor bearer really saying? He is saying, "Now, I see your vision, but your vision doesn't make much sense. I'm not sure I understand your vision, but I'm with you. I'm not with you because of the vision, because it is kind of wacky. Yet I'm coming with you, and I'm staying with you,

> I'm coming with you, and I'm staying with you, I'm following you, not so much because of the clarity of your vision, but because of the character of your heart.

I'm following you, not so much because of the clarity of your vision, but because of the character of your heart. I trust you. I stand with you. I will stay with you. I'm going with you because I'm trusting your heart."

Let us explain a truth to you. When you're leading a ministry, church, or organization, you don't always know what is next. You don't always know where to turn. You don't always know what's coming down the line. There are times when your people are following you, and you don't always know where you are going. It is in those times that your people will continue to follow you if they know your heart and can trust you. It is extremely important that you convey your heart all along the way so that in the darkest of times, your people can trust your heart even when they can't catch your vision.

More Important than Sharing Your Vision: Sharing Your Heart

I (Kenneth Ulmer) used to teach (as many other leadership gurus) that the most important issue in leading is *vision*. More than anything else, and sequentially, the first and most important thing is to share the vision. I can remember teaching, preaching, and lecturing on leadership, and time and time again, I would prioritize the need to share your vision. I have since adjusted my philosophy. Now I suggest this principle: *more important than sharing your vision is the priority of sharing your heart*. If followers have your heart, they can catch your vision. However, if they catch your vision without catching or before they catch your heart, they will more times than not distort or corrupt that vision. They can have your vision without having your heart. The result can often be tragic.

I am thinking of a dear friend, a great leader of a great church. He led a magnificent staff of gifted and anointed men and women. After several years, one of his staff members got the "itch" to pastor and lead his own congregation. Subsequently, he planted a church not very far from his home church. Interestingly enough, he planted that church with hundreds of members from his home church. Such unfortunate scenarios happen all too often in the Body of Christ.

I think the unique aspect of this example is that the young pastor's new congregation was built on many of the components, emphases, and priorities of his previous place of ministry. He had caught the vision of his former pastor. He had caught the vision of the former church structure and organizational systems. He had caught the man's vision, but he did not have his heart. The split in the church was painfully traumatic to his former church home. In fact, several of the key leaders went with him to the church plant.

Again, I readily acknowledge the frequency of such incidents, but when I look at the pain, disappointment, and friction between the two congregations, I think, "He had his pastor's vision; but he did not have his pastor's heart." The vision was distorted into another schism in the Body. Okay, I know the sovereign Lord always has the last word in such cases, but I think it is another example of a vision distorted and a heart rejected.

When a person on your team has your heart, that person may not always understand or see you vision, but he or she stands with you, supports you, and prays for you because he or she knows your heart. Over and over, we see examples of great biblical kings who had a grip on the vision of national leadership without having the spiritual heart of their fathers.

Two such examples are found in the blood line/king line of Judah. Hezekiah is identified as a man who "did that which was right in the sight of the Lord, according to all that David his father did" (2 Kings 18:3). He ruled with both the spiritual heart and political vision of his forefather, David. By the way, note that he followed the vision of an imperfect patriarch, but one whose heart had been cleansed and anointed by his God (Ps. 51). However, Hezekiah's son, Manasseh, proved to have the political ambitions and monarchial vision of his father, but he clearly lacked the spiritual commitment and righteous heart of the father, Hezekiah.

Biblical names always fascinate me. I am never sure if the names are prophetic or historical. Is it interesting that Hezekiah named his son Manasseh, which means forgetfulness, he that has forgotten! (*Hitchcock Biblical Names Dictionary*). Manesseh clung to his father's vision of leading the nation of Judah and the people of God but seemed to have "forgotten" his father's heart for the things of God, as displayed by his trust in the Lord God of Israel and his steadfast commitment to follow the Lord (2 Kings 18:5–6).

Now let's go back to that passage in Habakkuk.

When your congregation or fellow leaders know your heart, they will trust you when there is confusion all around or the plan does not make sense to them. When they don't know what is coming next, they will trust your heart if you spend time sharing your heart with them. Remember, they can only know your heart if you share it! When they have questions and you don't have answers, they will trust your heart because the Scripture says, "'I'm with you,' he says, 'according to your heart.'" This is what it means to be baptized into the visionary, not the vision.

You've been baptized into a visionary who was led by a vision. That vision is not a snapshot, freezing a moment in time. It is an ongoing revelation of God's will for your life. In Isaiah 43:19, we read, "Behold, I will do a new thing; now it shall spring forth; shall ye not know it? I will even make a way in the wilderness, and rivers in the desert." He is saying, "I'm doing a new thing."

> God has sovereignly ordained your steps to bring you to this new place in time that he might do in your life and through your life, a new thing.

God's Vision Is a New Thing

The vision is a new thing. What God has revealed is His vision to the man of God or the woman of God, for their community and for their lives; it is a new thing. God has sovereignly ordained your steps to bring you to this new place in time that he might do in your life and through your life, a new thing. God has brought you here for such a time as this, to be a part of something supernaturally new.

There are two major words for "new" in Scripture. One means "new in time," and one means "new in kind." God says, "I'm going to do a new thing."

Imagine Elise, who is a worship leader at a thriving local church. She currently drives a 2016 Volkswagen. One week, Elise goes to her church. Although her 2016 Volkswagen sounds new, there is a new set of keys waiting for her.

When she goes into the office, her pastor gives to her a set of keys to a new car. She says to her friends, "I have a new car." She leads her friends to the parking lot, and now she has a brand-new 2017 Volkswagen, with only three miles on it. Elise has a new car "in time," but not "in kind."

Let's rewind this imaginative situation. Elise comes in the next Sunday and is given keys for a new car. She says, "Praise the Lord. Praise the Lord. Praise the Lord. God's given me favor. I got a new car!" Elise then leads her friends out to the parking lot, and there is a brand-new 2017 Mercedes Benz. She had a 2016 Volkswagen, but now she has a new car—not just new "in time," but new "in kind." It's not just an upgraded,

> When you come into the power and the presence of the living God, all things are passed away, and all things become new. Your eyes have not seen. Your ears have not heard.

remodeled version of her old car. It's something totally brand new that she's never seen before!

What God wants to do in our lives and ministries is to do a new thing, not just a warmed-over, revised version of what we used to be. When you come into the power and the presence of the living God, all things are passed away, and all things become new. Your eyes have not seen. Your ears have not heard. We cannot imagine in our minds the great things God wants to do that are not just new in time but new in kind! God has a vision to lead your ministry and wants to show you the new—in time and in kind.

Yet, often with this new "in time" vision, problems and persecutions will come our way. Moses knew what the vision of his generation was for Israelites to exit from Egypt. However, Moses would not be able to possess this vision and pace it through the fathers of Israel without first engaging in a fight with Pharaoh. In fact, ultimately it was the sovereign hand of God that brought Israel out of Egyptian bondage.

Twelve Steps of a Vision's Manifestation

We wish to suggest that there are twelve steps from having the vision in your heart to holding the vision in your hand. As you will note in these twelve steps, there comes a time when pain and persecution become realities before the visionary leader fulfills his or her divine destiny. This is a sort of "rite of passage" for the process of leadership baptism.

1. **Give your vision a birth date.** *The vision must be born from within.* Your vision must a have a birthdate, a beginning date. You must know that *you know* the vision is from the Lord and that He has assigned you to fulfill it. If you do not have the inner fortitude that the vision is definitely from the Lord, then when the storms comes you will believe your doubts and doubt your beliefs. Do you know the place where the Lord gave you the vision? Can you take us back to that place? Can you still feel the faith that welled up in your heart when the vision was birthed in your heart?

2. **Subscribe.** *The vision has to be owned.* The leader reads and studies all the elements relating to the vision. Until you take ownership of that which has been given to you, you will never move from a man's day-dream to a God-sized vision. Throughout the entirety of this book, we have been advocating that first the leader possesses the vision, and then the vision possesses the leader.

3. **Inscribe.** *The vision must be written.* The greatest visions are written into short, pithy statements. Short does not mean shallow. Until you are able to write it down in concise wording, your vision will not be clear to you and others. Write it down so you can run with it. When

Moses came down from Mount Sinai, he brought God's vision with him for his generation in the form of ten short commandments. What is the summary of the vision? Write it down. What are the desired outcomes of the vision when it is fulfilled? Write them down. You will probably have to write the vision several times until every word is filled with a clear meaning.

4. **Describe.** *The vision must be shared with key partners.* Until the God vision is shared with others, you will not be able to build and broaden a net that works. The more on ramps you can create for others to get on the highway of your vision, the more significantly people will support you in the fulfillment of this vision. In the early days, keep the vision to yourself until you know you can trust the people around you. Learn from the mistake of Joseph sharing the vision with his brothers!

5. **Prescribe.** *The vision must have steps for the involvement of partners.* Think of this involvement in terms of information, interaction, investment, and integration. As visionary leaders, we have to lead people through personalized phases for them to be ultimately baptized into visionary leaders and into the vision. People come to a project from different angles; they need different doors to walk through to achieve divine fulfillment in their lives.

6. **Expect persecution.** *The vision will be attacked by others with different agendas.* Sooner or later, the visionary and the vision will come under attack. I am not sure that you can prevent it. Even the best-prepared leader cannot discern the wolves from the sheep every time. Dr. Leonard Sweet of SpiritVenture Ministries in New

Jersey has often said, "Where the Lord builds a church, Satan builds a chapel. Where the Lord is with His disciples, there usually is a Judas in the midst of them." The Bible is filled with numerous examples of visionary leaders eventually undergoing persecution.

7. **Anticipate betrayal.** *The vision will be betrayed by some who claim to be allies.* There is something exceptionally deep about this. The greatest battles are not fought outside of our circle but inside our circle. When you are in doubt about someone, be careful what you say and do. There is much personal, emotional pain when betrayal takes place in the inner circle of the visionary leader's life. While you are assessing your enemies, you'd better take extra care to assess your friends.

8. **Conquer death.** *The vision must die to be powerful.* This is the most painful time in a visionary's life. You may end up feeling all alone and wonder if you, and the vision, will live again. Start climbing out of the grave! Keep on doing what the Lord has commanded you to do. The greatest conqueror of criticism is success! The vision has been birthed by God. It will not be dead for a long period of time. During this midnight hour of the visionary's soul, the leader will come to realize that the burden of the vision is just as real as it has ever been in his or her life.

> **The greatest conqueror of criticism is success!**

9. **Celebrate resurrection:** *The vision will become more powerful than before.* Death and resurrection bring greater influence and more results. Your critics will dance at your apparent death, but when the Lord resurrects you and the vision, it will demonstrate the

power and plan of Christ to them and the world. You will be resurrected in your personal emotions, mental capacity, spiritual influence, and financial well-being.

10. **Gather provision:** *The vision has greater provision than ever.* People of provision who were watching in the past will begin to give generously for the vision to be fulfilled in this generation. These financial outsiders will become convinced that the visionary leader has the wherewithal to see this vision through to its completion. At this phase, it is far easier to ask for larger donations than at any previous time. The higher the respect, the higher the revenue!

11. **Allow the vision to speak for itself.** *The vision now speaks for itself.* Now people are talking about what the vision is accomplishing, without the visionary leader doing all the communicating. Testimonies come after the test. When you pass the vision test, people will begin talking about what the Lord is doing, even when you are not talking about it at all. At this point on the faith-filled journey, you will not need to go "everywhere" for there to be great success.

12. **Watch it multiply.** *The vision has moved from addition to multiplication.* All future planning is built on multiplication-focused thinking and execution for compounding results. This is the time when visionaries commit the rest of their lives to *reproducing* instead of just *producing*. Your every assignment is now viewed through this lens of acceptance and application.[24]

---

[24] Davis, James O. *How To Make Your Net Work: Tying Relational Knots For Global Impact.* Pp 110-11. 2013

We encourage you to take the time to ponder and pray over these twelve steps. After all, the greatest visionary leader of all time, Jesus Christ, was born, persecuted, died, resurrected, and multiplied His vision to live eternally!

Vision Is Seasonal

Finally, please note that vision is seasonal. We will spend a little more time and expand on this very critical dimension of vision. Vision is seasonal.

The vision is for a season. There is a time and season for everything under the sun (Eccl. 3:1). Vision is often relegated to a particular season. For every vision, there is a fresh anointing to fulfill that vision for that season. In Psalm 92:10, the psalmist says, "But my horn shalt thou exalt...I shall be anointed with fresh oil." Two revelations come forth from this text. First, the horn symbolizes strength, courage, and victory over the opposition of the enemy. Fresh oil speaks of oil that comes from freshly harvested pure, new olives. Also, the idea of being anointed with fresh olives and new strength implies a new season.

David was anointed three times, each for a new dimension of God's call in his life. The first time, he was anointed by Samuel and received power and strength to kill a bear, a lion, and a giant (1 Sam. 16:13). Second, he was anointed ruler over Judah, one tribe (2 Sam. 2:1–4). Finally, he was anointed a third time as king over all Israel (2 Sam. 5:3). Clearly, each level of anointing required a new vision. From slaying enemies in the flesh to ruling one tribe, Judah, David ruled in the dimension of praise. "Judah" means praise. Then he moves to the fulfillment of prophetic proclamation as ruler over the entire nations of twelve tribes—a new anointing for a new season.

Another clue about the seasonal character of vision is seen in the very title of Psalm 92. It is labeled "A Psalm or Song for the Sabbath." It would have been a section in Israel's hymnbook with songs sung specifically at the Sabbath worship. "Sabbath" means seventh. It marks that seventh day on which God rested after creation. However, the seventh day is not only a day that culminates in and reflects on the previous "season" of the past week. It is also the day before the eighth day, the day of new beginnings. It's the day that marks the end of one season and the beginning of a new season.

God gives a fresh anointing for every new season. And with every new season, He gives a fresh vision. For every appointment, God gives a fresh anointment. His visions are released for a set season, a set period of time, and then He moves you into the next season. Moses fought with people who continued to cling to and long for the past season of Egypt. Repeatedly they cried out to go back to the old season and the old provisions. As you read this book, please never forget: that you never want to be where God was!

There again is the lesson of snapshot vs. video! God had a vision for the season of the snapshot, but He does not remain there. Many are holding on to the vision of a season that is gone and over. Our prayer for you is that you would receive a fresh anointing for your new season and the vision God will give you that affirms your victory.

Visionary Leader Spotlight: William Borden

In 1904, William Borden graduated from a Chicago high school. As heir to the Borden family fortune, he was already wealthy. For his high school graduation present, his parents gave sixteen-year-old Borden a trip around the world. As the young man traveled throughout Asia, the Middle East, and Europe, he felt a growing burden for the world's hurting people. Finally, Bill Borden wrote home about his "desire to be a missionary."

One friend expressed disbelief that Bill was "throwing himself away as a missionary."

A story often associated with Borden says that, in response, he wrote two words in the back of his Bible: "No reserves."

Even though young Borden was wealthy, he arrived on the campus of Yale University in 1905 trying to look like just one more freshman. Very quickly, however, Borden's classmates noticed something unusual about him—and it wasn't that he had lots of money. One of them wrote, "He came to college far ahead, spiritually, of any of us. He had already given his heart in full surrender to Christ and had really done it. We who were his classmates learned to lean on him and find in him a strength that was solid as a rock, just because of this settled purpose and consecration."

During his college years, Bill Borden made an entry in his personal journal that defined what his classmates were seeing in him. That entry said simply, "Say 'no' to self and 'yes' to Jesus every time."

Borden's first disappointment at Yale came when the university president spoke in a convocation about the students' need of "having a fixed purpose." After that speech, Borden wrote, "He neglected to say what our purpose should be, and where we should get the ability to persevere and the strength to resist temptations." Surveying the Yale faculty and much of the student body, Borden lamented what he saw as the end result of an empty, humanistic philosophy: moral weakness and sin-ruined lives.

During his first semester at Yale, Borden started something that would transform campus life. One of his friends described how it began:

It was well on in the first term when Bill and I began to pray together in the morning before breakfast. I cannot say positively whose suggestion it was, but I feel sure it must have originated with Bill. We had been meeting only a short time when a third student joined us and soon after a fourth. The time was spent in prayer after a brief reading of Scripture. Bill's handling of Scripture was helpful... He would read to us from the Bible, show us something that God had promised, and then proceed to claim the promise with assurance.

Borden's small morning-prayer group gave birth to a movement that soon spread across the campus. By the end of his first year, 150 freshmen were meeting weekly for Bible study and prayer. By the time Bill Borden was a senior, 1,000 of Yale's 1,300 students were meeting in such groups.

Borden made it his habit to seek out the most "incorrigible" students and try to bring them to salvation. "In his sophomore year, we organized Bible study groups and divided up the class of three hundred or more, each man interested taking a certain number, so that all might, if possible, be reached. The names were gone over one by one, and the question asked, 'Who will take this person?' When it came to someone thought to be a hard proposition, there would be an ominous pause. Nobody wanted the responsibility. Then Bill's voice would be heard: 'Put him down to me.'"

Borden's outreach ministry was not confined to the Yale campus. He cared about widows, orphans, and the disabled. He rescued drunks from the streets of New Haven. To try to rehabilitate them, he founded the Yale Hope Mission. One of Bill Borden's friends wrote that he "might often be found in the lower parts of the city at night, on the street, in a cheap lodging house or some restaurant to which he had taken a poor hungry fellow to feed him, seeking to lead men to Christ."

Borden's missionary call narrowed to the Muslim Kansu people in China. Once he fixed his eyes on that goal, Borden never wavered. He also challenged his classmates to consider missionary service. One of them said of him, "He certainly was one of the strongest characters I have ever known, and he put backbone into the rest of us at college. There was real iron in him, and I always felt he was of the stuff martyrs were made of, and heroic missionaries of more modern times."

Although he was a millionaire, Bill seemed to "realize always that he must be about his Father's business, and not wasting time in the pursuit of amusement." Although Borden refused to join a fraternity, "he did more with his classmates in his senior year than ever before." He presided over the huge student missionary conference held at Yale and served as president of the honor society, Phi Beta Kappa.

Upon graduation from Yale, Borden turned down some high-paying job offers. It has been reported that in his Bible, Bill Borden wrote two more words: "No retreats."

William Borden went on to do graduate work at Princeton Seminary in New Jersey. When he finished his studies at Princeton, he sailed for China. Because he was hoping to work with Muslims, he stopped first in Egypt to study Arabic. While there, he contracted spinal meningitis. Within a month, twenty-five-year-old William Borden was dead.

When the news of William Whiting Borden's death was cabled back to the United States, the story was carried by nearly every American newspaper. "A wave of sorrow went around the world...," one headline read. "Borden not only gave (away) his wealth, but himself, in a way so joyous and natural that it (seemed) a privilege rather than a sacrifice," wrote Mary Taylor in her introduction to his biography.[25]

Was Borden's untimely death a waste? Not in God's perspective. As the story has it that prior to his death, Borden had written two more words in the back of his Bible. Underneath the words "No reserves" and "No retreats," he is reported to have written "No regrets."[26]

Dr. Ronnie Floyd, Lead Pastor of Cross Church in Springdale, Arkansas, summed it with:

We can all get in the mode of playing it safe in life. We tend to retreat from those things that are hard. When we look back over time, we often have many regrets. How will you live your life? Will you give 1,000 percent despite the challenges that may come your way? Live life with the following:

- **No reserves.** Do *not* hold back. Whatever it is or whatever you are facing, do not hold back. Face it. Go for it.

- **No retreats.** Do *not* always choose the easy path. There are times when God's will is not easy. o not turn back. Go forward with God.

> No retreats. Do not always choose the easy path. There are times when God's will is not easy. Go forward in what God is leading you to do in life. Do not turn back. Go forward with God.

---

[25] http://home.snu.edu/~hculbert

[26] No Reserves. No Retreats. No Regrets. Daily Bread, December 31, 1988, and The Yale Standard, Fall 1970 edition.

Go forward in what God is leading you to do in life. Do not turn back. Go forward with God.

- **No regrets**. Do *not* live cautiously. When your life is over, have no regrets. Live life to the fullest. Choose only God's will.[1] As a visionary leader, live with no reserves, no retreats, and no regrets.

---

[1] Floyd, Ronnie. May 6, 2013 Blog. No Reserves, No Retreat, No Regret.

CHAPTER 6

THE VISIONARY POWER

We are not only baptized into a visionary role and vision, but into victory.

You are a visionary leader, a Moses, a God-ordained leader to lead your congregation or organization into the vision that God has revealed to you. You've been baptized into a vision that, although sometimes is cloudy and not clear, is a vision that takes you into something brand new. God wants to do something new in your life, not just a warmed-over, revised version of what you used to be. He wants to make you brand new and lead you into victory.

In Psalm 133:1, we read, "Behold, how good and how pleasant it is for brethren to dwell together in unity!" This passage continues with, "the precious ointment upon the head and the beard of Aaron."

Anointing Oil Flows Over the Leader

When we come together in a worship service, something happens in the spirit realm—a supernatural shifting takes place around us. When we come together in worship, we must understand that there's a shifting in the spirit realm. Something happens supernaturally when we come together in one accord, in one place. It is a release of the anointing of the presence of the living God. It's like the oil that is poured over the head of Aaron.

Aaron was the priest whose job it was to lead them into the presence of God. When you lead your people into the presence of God, there's a shift in the atmosphere, and it's like the anointing oil that's being poured out, as it was poured over the head of Aaron.

This anointing oil flows down over the head of the one who is leading his or her church or ministry into the presence of God. There's an anointing in your ministry, and it begins with the presence of God and the power of God flowing over your head to every part of the local church or organization. This glorious anointing flows down from the throne of God over the head of the leader into the lives of those who are connected with this man or woman of God, who will lead them into the things of God for victory. You have been baptized into victory.

> There's something about the anointing of God that brings you through the lowest point, the driest point, the hardest point, the saddest point...

This powerful anointing flows down, down, down, down. The Bible says the anointing flows over the head, over the garments, and "It gathers at the hem of the garment." It starts at the head and flows to the hem. The anointing of God is like the oil poured over the head that pours over the garment and flows down, down, down to the hem.

When they poured the oil, they would not pour it sparingly; they would pour it lavishly over the head. They would never wipe it off with a towel. They would pour it lavishly over the head, and it would flow down, down, down, down, down to the hem, which means that the greatest concentration of the oil is not on the head, but at the hem, the lowest point on the garment.

God's Power Flows into Our Lives at the Darkest Moments

The power of God that flows in your life does not manifest itself only when you're at your highest, tallest, or biggest moment in life! There's something about the anointing and power of God that kicks in when you're at the lowest point of your life and you don't know where to turn and don't know how to make it. It began when you were on the mountaintop, but it kicks in when you're in the valley. There's something about the anointing of God that brings you through the lowest point, the driest point, the hardest point, the saddest point, until you stand and give God praise and glory, and you give God a testimony because you remember how far He has brought you.

There are times in leaders' lives when God does more in a split second than could be recorded in entire volumes of books. In 1 Kings 19:19–21, we read that Elijah walks into an open field. Unannounced and without fanfare, he transfers his divine logo, his mantle, to the shoulders of Elisha. In this holy moment, God was saying more and doing more than then the largest, most comprehensive text could ever record.

Similarly, Jesus Christ would break bread, saying simply, "This is my body." However, He was also saying more and doing more in that moment than entire volumes of books could ever record. Going forth from the solemn night of ordination, God can and will do more than you could ever imagine.

Each of Us Must Find God's Unique Role for Us

God wants to lay something upon you for the assignment that He has for you. We may have different roles, but we all have the same goal—to reach everyone. Anything less than a goal that involves everyone is not a God-sized goal. God is not interested in just a percentage of the world. He is interested in the whole world.

That goal is too big for you, and that goal is too big for me. We all have a role in the goal; we all have a part in God's heart. My role may be one way, and your role may be different, but the same touch of God that comes upon me is the same touch of God that comes upon you to fulfill the roles that God has for us.

But how can we discover our own role? How do we get on the right pathway? And how do we walk it out each day of our lives? It's imperative to find this pathway and, in the process, use the incredible power and grace that is ours through God.

We Have a Priority to Practice

First of all, we *have a priority to practice*. Elisha ministers unto his master Elijah. As ministers under our Master Jesus, our first priority is to minister to the King of the universe. That's our first priority. It's not to your church; it's not to my church. When we say, "Well, over at my church we do this and we do that," we need to remember that it is not our church; it is His church. It's HIS church. He has given us the privilege to serve and to minster unto Him.

If our first priority is to minister unto our Master, what kind of ministry did Elisha have? He washed the hands of his master. How long did he do that? He did it for eight years. He washed the hands of his master. Any time Elijah's hands got dirty, Elisha's responsibility was to wash his hands.

If we were to post on your organization's website, "By the way, we need men and women to help wash some hands," would we get much of a response? You can be too big for God to use, but you'll never be too small for God to use. God wants to use every one of us. But sometimes we let our egos get in the way. Someone has wisely defined "ego" to mean simply "Edging God Out." We've got to make sure that we are faithfully ministering to our Master.

We are to begin our day with Him; we are to end our day with Him. We are to walk and talk with Him and make sure that He gets all the glory and all the honor. If that is our priority, God will empower us. God will anoint us each day of our lives. We are not to be wandering generalities. We are to be definite specifics. We are to know God's plan. We are to get on the path and not chase every bouncing bunny rabbit or every opportunity that comes our way.

It's important to remember that every opportunity isn't necessarily God-sent. Every ordained minister must have discernment to stay on the path so that God will continue to bless his or her ministry and life. This doesn't mean you won't necessarily have challenges. Problems will come your way as well. But we have a priority to practice, and we are to make sure that our preaching, our teaching, our leadership, and our partnerships bring glory and honor to the Lord.

> God wants to use every one of us. But sometimes we let our egos get in the way.

We Have a Price to Pay

Second, *we also have a price to pay.* Power with God is not without cost. Everybody wants to do the extraordinary. Everybody wants to be in the "A game," whatever that may be. But to get in the A game, there's a price to pay.

Elisha had to pay the price when Elijah laid the mantle on him. It cost him his private relationships. In truth, I'm a much better husband when Jesus Christ is number one in my life than when He is number two in my life. There is one place where Christ will not work, and that's in second place. He is not looking for a diminished place in our lives. He's looking for the position of number one. As men and women of God, we are to be in a first-love relationship with Jesus every day until we die or until He comes back for us. If we love the Lord less today than we did yesterday, we have backslidden that far.

You and I know this is also true in our earthly friendships. We attract who we are, not what we want. If we are attracting lukewarm, lackadaisical, compromising people around us, we need to pause long enough to ask why we are attracting these kinds of people. I want to caution every candidate for ministry to choose his or her friends carefully. I can promise you this—some of the friends you start with are friends you will not finish with. As you follow Christ on your journey, you will wonder why this one goes one way,

> There is one place where Christ will not work, and that's in second place. He is not looking for a diminished place in our lives. He's looking for the position of number one.

and this one goes another way, why this one backslides and goes off the cliff that way, and somebody goes over the cliff a different way. Making wise choices in relationships is vitally important. In fact, how and why you end a relationship can be more important than how and why you start one. The important thing is this: No matter what others do, each candidate for ministry must keep his or her eyes on the Master.

However, we all need certain people in our lives. We need friends who are sounding boards, people in our lives with whom we can unpack our luggage for those times when we have a bad day. Somebody is going to upset your plans; somebody is going to do the unthinkable. You might say, "That hasn't happened to me." Well, life's not over yet. Be forewarned; it will happen. A wise friend can be a valuable sounding board, especially during hard times.

Besides friends who are sounding boards, we also need springboards. These people know us well enough to see past the surface to understand our hearts. These people could also be called "second-milers." These people pull us up. The first mile is the trial mile; the second mile is the "smile mile." We need those friends who will help us get on the second mile because that's where the real victory is. We need people who will encourage us, build us up, and help us to be larger in our hearts and larger in our lives. We need people to expand our spirits, to help us dream dreams we have never dreamed, and to believe God for things we've never believed Him for.

I'll tell you what else we need—we need surfboards in our lives. We need people on the edge. We need people who will stretch us in our thinking. We need people who will cause us to pray differently than we've ever prayed before. We each have a call to fulfill individually. However, a "surfboard" kind of relationship throughout our spiritual journey as preachers and teachers, as men and women of God, will elevate us to new vistas in Christ. Our "surfboard" friends are vital. Remember, too, that if a friend falls, don't shoot him. Find a way to help him up. Private relationships are a form of personal wealth greater than money.

Elisha was a very wealthy young man destined to inherit his father's business. We used to sing a song many years ago: "The cross before me, the world behind me." Personal acquisitions are hard to let go. But Elisha knew he had to let go of his riches. He had to say, "There's something greater than what I have now."

He also had to let go of professional responsibilities. He was not only going to inherit his father's business; he'd also already been the manager and the supervisor. Besides his future inheritance, Elisha had to let his current, prestigious responsibility go in favor of a more lowly job. He had to be willing to say, "Lord, if you want me to wash hands, that's what I'll do. I'll wash hands."

Elisha went back to tell his parents that he was leaving. He didn't go back and ask for permission. He just said, "I'm leaving." His ordination became a celebration for him. Well, we ought to celebrate what God does in our lives, and as leaders, people will know what we appreciate based on what we decide to celebrate. In the heat of summer, we celebrate the blessing of air conditioning. In the winter, we celebrate the blessing of heat, but, my friend, there'll be something greater that we celebrate than these. As leaders in ministry, we celebrate the souls that come to Christ and the families that are changed by our calling to ministry.

People know what we appreciate by looking at what we celebrate. There's a price to pay and I challenge every one of us to pay that price because there are no shortcuts in the long run. We have to train in order to gain. We have to pay the price to make progress. We need to spend time with the right people so that we don't

> As leaders in ministry, we celebrate the souls that come to Christ and the families that are changed by our calling to ministry.

repeat the same mistakes over and over again. Let others go to the school of hard knocks; you don't have to go. Learn from them and grow and mature. There is a price to pay.

We Have a Path to Pursue

Besides a priority to practice and a price to pay, third, *we have a path to pursue*. At the beginning of 2 Kings is a very familiar story. Elijah and Elisha are walking together. They have a very close relationship with special conversations nobody else is having. They start at Gilgal, continue to Bethel, and then on to Jericho, and finally to the other side of the Jordan River. As they are walking to each place, Elijah would say to Elisha, "Stay here while I go on." Elisha's response was always the same: "As long as God lives and you live, I will never, ever forsake you." At each place, this is the scenario.

Now, why do you think Elijah tells Elisha to stay in the previous place while he goes on? He does it to find out whether or not Elisha is resolute enough to finish what he starts. He wants to know Elisha's level of follow-through. Follow-through is so important. To stay on an assignment through thick and thin, through easy and hard, through sickness and in health is follow-through.

So Elijah and Elisha are traveling along and having a conversation. They start at Gilgal, the *place of beginnings*. We've all had a place of beginnings. For me it was on July 15, 1973 B.C., when I came to know Jesus Christ as my personal savior. All of us start at B.C.—before Christ. Accepting His saving grace becomes the Gilgal for every Christian.

Once you know that you know that you know, then you don't go back and revisit it when the rain is coming down and the storm is blowing. You just know that you know. Once you settle it, there is something that swells up in your heart. Even when a baby dies, or some other tragedy happens, you are still believing

> **You have the certainty that God is taking care of you, God is molding you, God is shaping you.**

that God is working it all out. You have the certainty that God is taking care of you, God is molding you, God is shaping you. He's making you a man of God. He's making you a woman of God. We all need a Gilgal, a place of beginning.

The next place Elijah and Elisha visit is Bethel, *the place of breaking*. This world throws away broken things, but God uses broken things. The blessings come after the breaking. Go back and read church history; go back and read the Old Testament and the New Testament. Every man and woman of God at some time has a midnight hour when he or she has "to walk it out" in darkness until the sun comes up again. It's a place of breaking. You may say, "Well, that's not going to happen to me." Don't send me a text on the day it does. I'm telling you ahead of time—the place of breaking will come.

You might say, "Well, I'm not afraid of the devil." That is not even the question. The question is whether or not the devil is afraid of you. The truth is that you can get on God's path and plan to fulfill God's goal for you, but, at some time or another, you are going to meet a two-legged devil that's dressed up like a sheep. And if you don't have discernment, you will fail to realize that it's a wolf in sheep's clothing. The devil will put these wolves in your path to discourage you, distract you, and get you headed down the wrong road. There's a price to pay. There is a pathway and a time when you'll have to endure a breaking.

When Elijah and Elisha get to Jericho, they find it to be *a place of battles*. Elijah says to Elisha, in essence, "I had an Ahab, and I had a Jezebel. You are going to have an Ahab and a Jezebel, too. You are going to have some people who are going to love you; you are going to have people who despise you. You are going to have days when things are great and days when things are not great in the midst of the battles."

God Saves the Best for Last for His Servants

Finally, the two friends get to the River Jordan, *the place of beholdings*. You know, God saves the best for last. He's saving the best for his servants until the last. We are not trying to get to the front of the line. The greatest value is those who are at the end of the line, adding value to everybody else. We are not trying to be the first zero after the one. Why settle for that? Think about ten notches forward, and you'll find compounding value. A hundred million, a billion, ten billion? Wow! What a difference one zero can make when it's placed at the end! That's the reward associated with leadership baptism.

The place of beholdings has great promise. God has some phenomenal things planned for your life, for your family, and for your ministry. You may not see it in the first year, or even at five years, ten years, or twenty years. But every day you sow your seed. Then you sow it again and again, and you water it, and you sow more seed. Based on God's Word, I promise you'll have a compounded harvest down the road.

My friend, there is a pathway to pursue, but along the way are about four hundred other guys. These four hundred guys are making fun of Elisha. They say things like, "Hey, big boy, you are not going to be much when Elijah has taken flight.

> **The place of beholdings has great promise. God has some phenomenal things planned for your life, for your family, and for your ministry.**

You do know that God is going to take him away soon, right? And the only reason that you have any inside scoop is because he likes you, because you have favor in Elijah's eyes. But when he's gone, what are you going to have?" To our great surprise, Elisha looks at these mockers and says, "Be quiet." Another translation records a bolder response: "Shut up!"

Elisha doesn't engage them any further in conversation. If you don't have time to answer a critic's second e-mail, don't answer the first one because the critics have mastered criticism. The cynics have mastered cynicism. A book published several years ago is titled *Learning to Swim with the Sharks*. Marketers call this book factual. I call it fictional. You don't learn to swim with the sharks. In actuality, if you swim with the sharks, most likely they will have you for dinner. They ought to rename the book *Learn How to Have Dinner with the Sharks, and You're It*.

What's the solution to this problem? Stay on the shore. Invite the sharks there. Let's see how well that turns out for them. On the shore, you are operating from your strength, not your weakness. Similarly, if you wallow with the pigs in the mud, the pigs will have fun, but you won't enjoy it. Are we going to wallow with pigs, or are we going to soar with eagles? How are you going to live your life in ministry? If you please the Lord, it doesn't matter whom you displease. But if you displease the Lord, it doesn't matter whom you please. Stay on the path where you have strength for ministry.

We are not competing in a popularity contest. We are not trying to make everybody like us. We are simply preaching and teaching the Word of God and living an example that matches it. In the process, not everyone will always speak positively about you. In fact, having people speak positively of

> As a pastor, as a fellow minister, I challenge you to intentionally cross the street and meet other ministers and pastors. It may not be popular, but it might well advance the Kingdom in ways you have not yet seen.

you is not necessarily a compliment if you're not making a dent in their darkness.

What does Elisha do? He just says, "Hey guys, be quiet," because he has a relationship. All the other prophets knew was reputation. However, Elisha didn't know just reputation; he also knew relationship. They knew *about* Elijah, but he *knew* Elijah. The closer you get to the Lord, when the barrage of critics come—and they will—you just keep your eyes on your Master.

You might say, "That sounds easy." No, it is not. Sometimes criticism will come because others don't like when we "cross-pollinate" in and out different streams of Christianity. Some people think you should never, ever get "outside your tribe." However, I'm here to tell you, if you are going to finish the Great Commission, it's going to take more than your tribe.

You'll miss the mark if you operate only in your stream of Christianity. As a pastor, as a fellow minister, I challenge you to intentionally cross the street and meet other ministers and pastors. It may not be popular, but it might well advance the Kingdom in ways you have not yet seen.

We Have a Promise to Possess

Last, there is also *a promise to possess*. Elijah and Elisha continue their conversation on the other side of the river. I especially love this because it holds so much power and hope. Elijah says to Elisha, "Ask anything of me." Wow! If God whispered to you tonight and said to you, "Ask me for anything!" what would you say? You might say, "I'll ask Him for a piece of land." Well, that's great, but remember that he's God; he's Almighty God.

At the time of this writing, the richest person on the planet is worth seventy billion dollars. If you asked him, "Hey, can I borrow ten dollars?" he probably would not give you the money. You know why? He'd probably be insulted and say, "You don't even know who you are talking to. Your request is too small. You could have asked me for a billion."

When we come to God, we should ask Him for something big. Bill Bright used to tell me, "It's a compliment to God when you ask Him for something that only He can do." There used to be a time when we regularly asked God for our city. I don't hear many preachers today ask God for their city, let alone begin working on a strategy and a plan by which to do it. We don't ask God for our city. In fact, we ought to ask Him, "God, give us the whole state." You might say, "Well, that seems awfully hard." Really? We have this idea that it was easy for us to come to Jesus. In actuality, the most challenging group for God to save is probably a roomful of ministers. If God can save us, he can save anybody, including a whole city or an entire state.

So Elijah says to Elisha, "Ask anything of me, and I'll do it." I wonder how many times I have ever asked something big enough for God's response to be, "Now that's significant." When Elisha asks for Elijah's mantle, Elijah says: "You've asked a difficult thing. You've asked a hard thing." I wonder if I've ever asked God for anything so big that he would reply, "Wow, that's a big request. That just might stretch us a little bit up here."

I think we ought to ask God for something dynamic enough in our ministries that God would bring the angels over and say, "Listen to this. This request is really a compliment because I'm the only one who can answer it. These people are asking for something way beyond their capability." I challenge every person to ask God for something that only God can do. Then when He does it, make sure He gets all the glory and all the honor.

Then Elisha says, and we are paraphrasing, "I've been thinking about it, and I'll tell you what I want. I want a double touch. I want a double anointing upon my life. Elijah, whatever power you've had, double it. Super-size it for me. I want a bigger divine touch upon my life than you have had. Elijah, I want that more than health, I want that more than wealth, I want that more than land, I want that more than oxen, I want that more than any inheritance, I want that more than compliments. I want that more than anything. I want a double touch on my life. Whatever makes you unique, just double it upon my life."

In the very same way, God wants to supersize your ministry. God desires to double-touch your life. He desires to lay a hand upon you that you will never forget, as long as you live. You'll look back one day and mark it as the moment when God laid that mantle upon you, when he anointed your life for service to do His will.

Elijah's reply to Elisha is this: "All you've got to do is keep your eyes on me." That's what he said. "If you keep your eyes on me when I leave, you'll have it." If Elisha slept near his master, undoubtedly, he kept one eye open and on him all night. Perhaps it's your time right now. Basically, you know what Elijah was saying? It was this: "Just keep doing what you are doing. Keep doing what you've been doing. You've kept your eyes on me. You didn't focus on the other four hundred guys. You kept your eyes on me. Now, just keep doing it!"

As Elijah starts making his way up into the air, the mantle comes down. Elisha picks up that divine logo, walks over, and slaps it against the Jordan River. The four hundred men scatter behind rocks, all acknowledging the same thing: "He has it now, the same touch that Elijah had. He has it now. He has power with Almighty God."

The first time somebody put the mantle on for Elisha was when Elijah offered an "apprenticeship" to him. The second time, Elisha put it on himself. He believed the promise, and he applied it to his life as Elijah ascended to heaven. There are only two ascensions in the Bible—one in the Old Testament and one in the New Testament. You might argue that there are actually three if you consider Enoch. No, there are just two. Enoch's translation was not an ascension. He walked with God, and then he wasn't. One day, God just said, in essence, "We're a lot closer to my house than yours. Let's just go home together." And Enoch was gone.

But Elijah, has an ascension in the Old Testament, and Jesus has an ascension in the New Testament, so there are just two ascensions. In the Old Testament, Elijah went up, and the mantle came down. In the New Testament, Jesus went up, and the Holy Spirit came down. In the Old Testament, Elijah went up, the mantle came down, and the servant went out. In the New Testament, Jesus Christ went up, the Holy Spirit came down, and the servants were sent out.

But it doesn't stop there. Elijah went up, the mantle came down, and as Elijah went up, Elisha did twice as many miracles as his master. In the New Testament, Jesus Christ went up, the Holy Spirit came down, the disciples went out, and the Bible says they did greater things than their master. It all started with that divine touch on their lives.

Jesus says, "If anyone is thirsty, let him come unto me and drink. And he that believes in me as the scripture has said, out of his innermost being shall flow rivers of living water." Jesus said, "If anyone is thirsty…" Ladies and gentlemen, there is a difference between thirstiness and emptiness. My car has been on "E" many times, not to indicate excellence, but to indicate emptiness. However, my car has never been thirsty, not one time. I've put in many gallons of gas over the years, but never one time did I put gas in because my car was thirsty.

Jesus didn't say to you or me, "If you are empty, come." He said, "If you are *thirsty*, come." Listen to this. As one preacher to another, the level of our thirst determines the level of our satisfaction. A shallow thirst doesn't take much to satisfy. A deep thirst is an entirely different matter. A deep thirst requires much more water, and we, as men and women of God,

> Ladies and gentlemen, there is a difference between thirstiness and emptiness. My car has been on "E" many times, not to indicate excellence, but to indicate emptiness.

need to cultivate a thirstiness in our lives for that divine touch every day. The Lord will quench this thirst in our ministry with a divine promise, with the power of the Holy Spirit. The anointing of God's Spirit upon our lives is worth more anything else. It's something that only God can do.

It is beyond what we can do. It is done only by God, but He desires to do that for you. He wants to supersize your anointing. He wants to double it, triple it, quadruple it in your life. If God has called you, a daily touch like this will sustain you throughout the entirety of your ministry. And, my dear friend, God has greater things for you than you have ever dreamed, greater than what you have ever imagined. He has a supersized anointing for you.

With leadership baptism, you have not only been baptized into a visionary role and into vision, but into *victory*. Our challenge is to cultivate a thirst for God's divine power. In the process, we have a priority to practice, we have a price to pay, we have a pathway to pursue, and we have a promise to possess. His touch, that divine mantle transferred to us, makes the eternal difference in our preaching, in our teaching, and in our ministry until Jesus comes.

Visionary Leader Spotlight: James Hudson Taylor

James Hudson Taylor was born on May 21, 1832, into a family that prayed together and spoke often of other countries in which people had not heard the Word of God. Yet when he was seventeen, he chose not to follow the God his family knew. The following is a personal account of what changed his life, as taken from one of his books, *A Retrospect:*[27]

> I had many opportunities in early years of learning the value of prayer and of the word of God; for it was the delight of my dear parents to point out that if there were any such being as God, to trust him, to obey him and to be fully given up to his service must of necessity be the best and wisest course both for myself and others. But in spite of these helpful examples and precepts, my heart was unchanged. Often, I had tried to make myself a Christian, and failing of course in such efforts, I began at last to think that for some reason or other I could not be saved, and that the best I could

---

[27] . James Hudson Taylor, *A Retrospect* (Charleston, S.C.: CreateSpace, 2015).

      do was to take my fill of this world, as there was
      no hope for me beyond the grave.

    During this time, Hudson Taylor and his friends were skeptical of Christianity and turned off by "the inconsistencies of Christian people" who claimed to believe the Bible but "were yet content to live just as they would if there were no such book." Taylor's mother and sister persisted in praying for him. In June 1849, just one month after his sister decided to pray for him daily, he had a change of heart through reading a small tract. This changed his understanding of the change that God brings and the completion of God's purpose through the life of Christ.

    Brought into saving faith through such a testimony, the power of prayer continued to be a valuable core of his life. He knew that "the promises were very real, and that prayer was in sober matter-of-fact transacting business with God, whether on one's own behalf or on behalf of those for whom one sought his blessing."

    In the following years of his life, through poor health, financial pinches, and completion of his medical studies, he became a missionary in China. He sailed on the *Dumfries* in September 1853 and landed in Shanghai on March 1 in the midst of a rebellion. As he spent time studying the language, he saw that many missionaries of his day had adopted rich lifestyles and that few had gone farther inland to the rural and poorer areas.[28]

    After six months, he moved to a little house where he could get to know his Chinese neighbors. One day, as he watched a fire from a little balcony, a cannonball hit a wall near him, showering him with tile bits and landing in the courtyard below. Taylor decided to move back to the foreigners' compound

---

[28] Reese, Ed. James Hudson Taylor. Wholesomewords.org/missions/biotaylor2.html.

just before his house was burned to the ground. His mother kept the four-to-five-pound ball for years as a small token of God's great protection of her son.

Together with his coworkers, Hudson Taylor began speaking, preaching, and distributing literature in nearby areas. However, when he saw that the Chinese people could only see him as an outsider he followed the example of Dr. Charles Gutzlaff, whom he called the "grandfather of the China Inland Mission," and chose to wear the clothes of the common Chinese people. Although this made him the laughingstock of both foreign and Chinese onlookers, the effects proved his point and helped people see that what he preached was not such a foreign message after all. As a result of Missionary Hudson choosing to wear the Chinese clothing of the people, he is now known as the "Father of Cross-Cultural Missions."

In 1857, Hudson Taylor resigned from the Chinese Evangelization Society, and he and a coworker founded a mission in Ningbo. The following year, he married Maria Dyer, the daughter of another missionary family. They had thirteen children (three of whom died at birth). In 1870, Maria became very ill and died. She is buried in China.

Hudson Taylor wanted to reach the Chinese in the rural and inland areas. He was convinced that a new mission was needed for the task. However, the idea of shouldering such a burden troubled him. Suddenly, while on Brighton Beach, a fresh truth dawned on him: the responsibility was not his, but God's! On the flyleaf of his Bible, he wrote, "Prayed for the 24 willing, skillful laborers at Brighton, June 25, 1865."

Please note carefully here that the burden became a vision. Next, Missionary Taylor began to reach out to other distinguished leaders, encouraging them to join him in this vision. (It is imperative for the visionary leader to possess the vision, pass on the vision, and then pace the vision.)

In 1865, Hudson Taylor founded the China Inland Mission (CIM). He knew that millions of people needed to hear the message of Jesus Christ and thus named the mission magazine *China's Millions*. It is published today as *East Asia's Millions*.

While stressing the need to preach widely, Hudson Taylor urged local churches to establish and mature; for church buildings to be of Chinese, not foreign, design; and for leaders of the churches to be Chinese Christians. His burden for the still-unreached areas pressed him further. The first party of eighteen sailed for China in 1866, and eighteen more sailed in 1870. In 1886, he issued another call for 100 new workers in two years; 102 were sent out by the end of 1887. In 1888, the first North American party was sent out.

Hudson Taylor was known as a man of prayer, just as he learned the power of prayer through his mother and sister. Also known as a "man of faith," he would respond that he was "only a servant of a faithful God." Hudson Taylor died on June 3, 1905, and was buried in Changsha, Hunan. The CIM, known for a time as the Overseas Missionary Fellowship and now OMF International, was thus established and supported through his example and his urgent requests for people to pray and go. May those of our generation uphold the Word of our faithful God, living, preaching, and praying according to His will, wherever we may be.

Because of the visionary leadership of James Hudson Taylor I, the Overseas Missionary Fellowship International has more than 1,300 full-time missionaries. It is estimated that the Christian population in China has grown to approximately 100 million! It is the largest community of Christians in a single nation.[29]

---

[29] James Hudson Taylor. Overseas Missionary Fellowship (OMFUSA.com)

CHAPTER 7

THE VISIONARY PATH

Three times in Exodus 14, the Word of God instructs us by saying that the Lord led them. Can you honestly say that you want the Lord to lead you? Sometimes the Lord leads us to the mountaintops where the eagles soar and at other times to the valleys where the scorpions roam. Sometimes He leads us to the sunshine and sometimes to the starlight. Can you honestly say that you want God to lead you? Leadership baptism creates in us a desire for God to lead us so we can then lead those who seek our capable direction.

Moses learned that the Lord delivered His people with great power (Ex. 14:31). Over and over, the psalmists refer to the Lord as a great God (Ps. 96:4; 145:3; 47:2; 48:2). Paul echoes the greatness of God. He speaks of the "exceeding greatness of his power to us-ward who believe, according to the working of his mighty power" (Eph. 1:19). In speaking of the greatness of God, Paul stacks synonyms one on top of the other. He uses four different words for "power," all of which carry nuances of the same power concept. His words (in the authorized version) are *dunamis, dynameōs, energeo, energeian, kratos, kratous, ischus, ischyos.*

All these words carry the meaning of power. We might paraphrase Paul's revelation as "the exceeding greatness of his power…according to the power of his powerful power." Paul speaks of the great power of a great God.

107

Grasp the Greatness of God

Dear friend, if you ever begin to grasp the greatness of your God, it can change your life. If you ever come to realize how great your God is, it will impact how big your dreams are. It will influence how big your goals are. It will inspire how big your vision is. You serve a great God. You serve a big God. God often invests great visions into those of great faith. Your visions become God-sized! Don't fear it. Don't back away from it. Embrace it. Prayerfully receive it. Faithfully walk in it. It is a God-sized vision from a great God!

Paul gives us insight into the practical spiritual paths of the visionary leader. He points out that Moses led the people "in the cloud and in the sea." God has called His leader to lead His people "on a path through the cloud and a path in the sea." We note that Israel followed the path "in" the sea in the sense that they walked through the bed of the sea, the

> If you ever come to realize how great your God is, it will impact how big your dreams are. It will influence how big your goals are. It will inspire how big your vision is. You serve a great God.

dry, dusty bottom of the sea while God parted the waters (Ex. 15:19). God made a highway through the waterway.

The Red Sea represents those obstacles that stand between you and God's destiny and His will for your life. Corporately, it represents the obstacles and challenges that can hinder God's people on their journey into the will of God. As a visionary leader, you will find yourself time and time again prayerfully leading the people of God through the obstacles and challenges of life. The lesson Moses teaches us is that we never face our Red Sea alone. This truth is seen in two scriptural pictures. First is the revelation of God's name, and the second in the request of Moses.

We are so much like Moses. We often focus on our weaknesses and overlook God's strength. We highlight our abilities—and the lack thereof—while God only wants our availability. Moses begins by questioning God's wisdom of choosing him by reminding God that he was a nobody. He had no reputation of being a man of authority. He had no name with any great pedigree or renown respectability. I love this exchange. In Exodus 3:13, Moses says, and we're paraphrasing, "Who shall I tell them sent me?" God responds by assuring Moses that He would be with him. Moses was a slow learner and retorted with the anticipation of being questioned about his name; in whose name would he come? "What name shall I use, Lord? My name has no power. My name cannot deliver these people. My name has no authority. I can't go in my name."

God said, in essence, "Try My name."

Moses responded, "What name shall I use? Who shall I say sent me?"

God said to Moses, "'I AM THAT I AM': and he said, 'Thus shalt thou say unto the children of Israel, I AM hath sent me unto you. Use my name, tell them, 'I AM THAT I AM; I AM sent you'" (Ex. 3:14). Victory for the visionary is in the name of God, I AM.

He did not say, "I WAS." "I" is not "I WILL BE." He is "I AM." He never was "was"; he never will be "will be." He is AM. It is the AM-ness of God that assures us of victory on the other side of our Red Seas. It is the IS-ness of God that leads us through the obstacles of our journey into His will. He dwells in the continual present tense. One of the greatest dangers of a visionary leader is to find himself or herself where God was! You never want to be where God *was*. He always *is*. He is always the I AM. Beware, my leader friend, that you don't waste your today holding on to your yesterday and miss your tomorrow.

Let's look closer at Moses's preparation to answer the call of God. He makes a reasonable request of God. He says, "Come with me." In fact, Moses says, in essence, "If you don't go with me, Lord, I'm not going."

In Exodus 33, Moses has another dialogue with the Lord. His request is interesting. He really wants to know God, and in his desire to know God, he makes the request for God to show him His ways. Moses knows that if he wants to know God better, he needs to know God's ways. He uses the most common word for "know" in Scripture. The Hebrew word *yada* is used in one nuance or another more than eight hundred times in scripture. The most applicable use of this word, as used by Moses, speaks of an experiential, intimate knowing. It is even used to depict sexual intimacy and represents an intimate knowing of God through the experiencing of His ways.

Moses had seen the ways of God. Moses was a prototype to the prophetic utterance of the prophet Isaiah hundreds of years later. Through Isaiah, God would say, "For my thoughts are not your thoughts, neither are your ways my ways, saith the LORD. For as the heavens are higher than the earth, so are my ways higher than your ways, and my thoughts than your thoughts" (Isa. 55:8–9).

The Visionary Leader's Path in the Sea

Moses had had a foretaste of God's ways already. Moses would realize that God had led him all the way by revealing His ways. Moses led the people of God through the obstacles of the Red Sea as an experience of God's ways. The very fact that they walked through the dry bed of the Red Sea is a revelation of the Ways of God. Probably the first expected method of crossing the Red Sea would have been in some type of water vehicle. Or at least a fleet of boats, ships. But enough boats for millions (so say some biblical historians)? I doubt it. And then if we had seen the power of God open the Red Sea with the breath of God, we would have been so excited about going through that we would have run into the bed of the sea and trudged through the muddy bottom. But God not only opened the sea; He made sure the bed of the sea was dry before His people made their trek to the other side. Moses would learn that God doesn't do things the way we do. He doesn't even think the way we do.

It is the "I AM" God who dwells in the eternal now-ness of His personhood. It is this same God Who says He will never leave you nor forsake you. One side of the promise is that God will never leave you behind; He will never run ahead of you. On the other hand, He will not stay behind and allow you to go into your tomorrow without Him. Stay with God, visionary leader. He will never leave you nor forsake you.

> He will never run ahead of you. On the other hand, He will not stay behind and allow you to go into your tomorrow without Him. Stay with God, visionary leader. He will never leave you nor forsake you.

Moses tried to give God a news flash. He questioned the Lord's wisdom in choosing him by informing God that he was not a good talker; in fact, he wanted God to know that he had a speech impediment.

The Visionary Leader's Path in the Cloud

The other path of the visionary leader is in the cloud. Under the cloud, in the cloud, under the protection of the cloud, guided by the cloud, led by the cloud. The visionary leader is called to lead the people of God on the path of the cloud. It is the path of God's glory. It is the path of God's guidance. It is the path of God's gracious presence.

Visionary leader, make it your priority—especially when the people of God gather corporately for worship—that you lead them into the glory presence of God. God promised Moses, "My presence shall go with thee, and I will give thee rest" (Ex. 33:14). That glorious presence of God was manifested at night as a pillar of fire, and by day it was a pillar of cloud. When they would pitch their tents and make camp, they rested in the glorious presence of God. However, when Moses led the people of God in the dedication of the tabernacle, the cloud of the Lord "christened" the place where He said He would meet with His people by hovering over their corporate gathering. They would move only when the cloud moved.

Beware, godly leader, that in your attempt to be culturally and contemporarily relevant, you don't leave out the priority of worship, to enter into the glory presence of God. The late Dr. Caesar Clark, a giant pillar of the African American pulpit, used to say, "Always leave room for Jesus on your program." We fear that, too often, the pressures of ministry are tempting many spiritual leaders to exorcise the glory of God from the highly programmed, often highly technological, expertly produced weekly gatherings of the people of God.

Our goal is to receive the glory of God. Never entertain a cloudless vision, a vision without the glory cloud of God. Many are choosing the crowd over the cloud. On His way to Calvary, Jesus reveals the divine strategy of His glorification and resurrection. He declared, "If I be lifted up, I will draw all *peoples* to Myself" (John 12:32, NKJV).

The glory of Jesus is the glory of the Father (John 8:54, NIV). When the soldiers lifted up Jesus, they were lifting up the glory of God. This is the essence of the Gospel. The Gospel is the Good News of the Savior's glory, the saving grace, and the sovereign goodness of God. It is this glory of Jesus that is the authentic Gospel.

The Attractiveness of Grace Often Comes at the Expense of Authenticity

Jesus said that He, through the glory of God, would draw all people unto Himself. It is the glorious power of God to draw, attract, influence, and induce people to come to Him. The glorious Gospel of the Kingdom is the authentic message of Jesus the Christ. That message has no authenticity outside of this glorious Savior. And it is the glory essence of the Christ that will attract and influence and draw people into the Kingdom of God.

In our attempts to lead the people of God on the path of the glory of God, we must be careful not to yield to the temptation of opting for attractiveness of that glory at the expense of its authenticity. This tension between the authenticity of the glorious Jesus and the attractiveness of that glory is not a choice of either/or; rather, it is a settled path of both/and—not either authenticity *or* attractiveness, but authenticity *and* attractiveness. Choosing one over the other is to prioritize the attracted crowd over the authentic cloud of the glory of the Son of God.

Many will opt for the authentic cloud of the glory of God. Their commitment to orthodoxy, tradition, and the historical elements of worship and the assembly of God's people will often manifest itself as "salt that has lost its savor."

Author and former pastor R. Kent Hughes speaks of the salt dynamic of the people of God. Hughes says one of the results of being salty is that "salt creates thirst. Jesus made people thirsty for God. Whenever anyone encountered Jesus, whether a Pharisee like Nicodemus or an outcast like Mary Magdalene, that person became thirsty for God. Are we salty enough to make people thirsty for Jesus?[30]"

---

[30] R. K. Hughes, *The Sermon on the Mount: The Message of the Kingdom* (Wheaton, IL: Crossway Books, 2001), 80.

Hughes addresses the inability of the church to influence and impact its culture:

> Is there such a thing as a desalted church? Our Lord indicates this is a possibility: *sus*, whether a Phari it saltiness. Some translations render this "tasteless." In actual fact, salt is an extremely stable compound and does not become taste-less. The consensus of most scholars is that Jesus is referring to its adulteration or dilution, which can happen in several ways that we will not go into. The point is, it is dangerously easy for Christians to lose their salty, preserving influence in the world. While many believers are pungent and salty, there are others who are virtually indistinguishable from the surrounding culture. I do not think any of us can look at professing Christianity at large or at American Christianity or at our local Christianity or at our own hearts without admitting that the possibility of saltless, insipid, bland Christianity is very real. The great tragedy is that often the world does us more harm than we do it good.[31]

The former pastor of the historic Tenth Presbyterian Church of Philadelphia, Pennsylvania, the late Dr. James M. Boice, notes that the fundamental characteristic of salt is to make one thirsty. He takes this issue to a more personal level:

> And this leads us to ask: Do you make anyone thirsty for Jesus Christ? The non-Christian tends to feel self-satisfied even if he is not, and he

---

[31] R. K. Hughes, *The Sermon on the Mount: The Message of the Kingdom* (Wheaton, IL: Crossway Books, 2001), 80.

naturally goes through life telling himself that circumstances are wonderful. But when a Christian comes into his sphere of vision, there should be that evidence of joy, satisfaction, and peace that makes him look up and say, "That's what I want; that is what I want to be like!" Can that be said of you? Do you make men thirsty for Jesus Christ?[32]

In some cases, the church is not making the crowd salty because of the distasteful nature of its vision. In some cases, it is the unpalatable way the cloud (the glory presence of God) is the glory pre-wrapped in the staid traditions, powerless liturgies, and structured, outdated methods of approaching the very presence of God that is, or should be, the goal of the gathering.

On the other hand, many choose the option of crowd over cloud. Most often, the gathering will compromise the power of the cloud in favor of the passions of crowd. Peter chose the anonymity in the crowd around the cross over his relationship with Christ on the cross. The rich young ruler chose the crowd of affluence over the denial required for the glory of the cross.

Others, in an attempt to be relevantly attractive, more times than not tend to dilute and water down the authentic Gospel of Jesus for fear of being "un-PC"—not politically correct, too condemning, too hard, cold, and uncompassionate.

The response of many church leaders to these changing times has been to lean toward being attractive at the sacrifice of authenticity. The authentic Christ is often sacrificed on the altar of cultural and political correctives. The goal of getting more seats filled within the walls of the church often

---

[32] . J. M. Boice, *The Sermon on the Mount: An Expositional Commentary* (Grand Rapids, MI: Baker Books, 2002), 65.

is attempted by presenting a savior whose concern is more for the now than the sweet by and by and whose coming was to save people from psychological and emotional scars rather than sin and its eternal consequences.

Pastors' sincere desire to please and honor the Lord often leads them to do whatever they can to grow the church—even if it means compromising their integrity, or worse, compromising the integrity of the Gospel and the identity of the Lord of the Gospel. It is this type of pastor who will often dilute the message of Christ and disguise the identity of Christ. By ignoring or distorting the primacy of Christ,

> The response of many church leaders to these changing times has been to lean toward being attractive at the sacrifice of authenticity. The authentic Christ is often sacrificed on the altar of cultural and political correctives.

pastors often hope that more people will be drawn to that house. Jesus becomes one of the great prophets. Jesus becomes the loving historical figure who speaks only positive blessings of prosperity, success, and unqualified health.

Striving for Success as a Leader Can Dilute the Biblical Truth

As the pendulum swings more and more toward success, Jesus becomes one of the paths to a loving God. Sin becomes a series of mistakes. Heaven becomes an earthly utopia, and salvation is more existential than spiritual, more of a universal reality rather than dependent on universal, potentiality-based repentance from sin and "calling upon the name of the Lord." Scams and schemes, false promises of earthly blessings, at best distort biblical truth, and worse present a Christless salvation that positions a relationship with God as a goal that is reachable by being a good person or choosing any one of the multitude of "optional paths" to

God. This was depicted on a marquee outside a church in downtown Los Angeles several years ago. The title of the next Sunday's message was "Many Paths Up the Same Mountain." This is extreme attractiveness that values not crossing the line of political correctness much higher than not crossing the lines of biblical hermeneutics, exposition, and the declaration that Jesus is "*the* Way, *the* Truth, and *the* Life".

In an attempt to draw crowds, preachers become motivational speakers rather than prophetic proclaimers of the Gospel of the Son of God Who came to die for the sins of the world. Sin is not attractive, and no one is attracted to a place where they are reminded that they are sinners. However, the truth is that sin is not a reference to our unholiness; it a reality that applies to "all" who "have sinned and come short of the glory (the cloud) of God "(Rom. 3:23, parentheses added).

By way of explanation, rather than defending this tension, I (Kenneth Ulmer) suggest this pull between the Glory Cloud of the Lord and the glittering crowd of the world might be paraphrased as a tension between the intoxication of success and the devastation of insignificance.

Every servant, leader, and child of God wants to one day hear the commendation of the Master: "Well done, good and faithful servant..." (Matt. 25:21). We want to do well. Our hearts truly desire to honor the Lord. But we are often so driven, so passionately consumed with hearing those words that we become so obsessed with success and aim for it at all costs. Sometimes it costs our integrity. Sometimes it costs our holiness. Sometimes it costs our reputation. Sometimes it costs our commitment to rightly dividing the Word of truth. We crave what we and others call success—and we strive for it by the Malcolm X philosophy: "by any means necessary."

When it appears that success is more and more elusive, in spite of sincere efforts and godly desire to honor the Lord, there is the ever-present tug and temptation to minimize the good work that has been accomplished in Jesus's name. Instead of looking up beyond the hills to the Lord Who is our help, eyes become fixed more on the bigger church down the street, the fancy ministry with all the bells and whistles of the televangelist where the crowds flock. The focus is drawn more to the bigger house down the street, and more likely to the people who pass your church on their way to that bigger place. They have more volunteers than you have members! You tend to diminish and devalue what God has done through you and deem it insignificant. This assessment of your labor is riddled with frustration and discouragement and is a recipe for depression. All too often, it adds to the growing number of people who leave the ministry every year. It is the devastation of insignificance.

It is often this dissatisfaction that makes the crowd more appealing than the cloud of the glory of God. This temptation of fame, success, notoriety, and acclaim was likened to the devil's tempting Jesus in the wilderness (Matt. 4:8–11). The devil took Jesus to a high mountain peak and showed Him the kingdoms of the world and its glory. He tried to make a deal with Jesus. He said he would give him all the kingdoms of the world. Wait. Hold it right there. This is Jesus. He is already King of Kings, and his Kingdom shall have no end! (Luke 1:33)

Do Not Bow to the Devil's Offers

Back to the story. OK, so the devil's deal is this: all the kingdoms would go to Jesus if He would "fall down and worship" the devil. Now, this temptation is not as cut and dried as you might think. No doubt you would not even entertain such an offer. Who would give up a life of serving the true and living God for living a life of worship and homage to the devil? But a close look reveals that the offer was a bit more complicated that a cut and dried dismissal of this life of ruling the kingdoms of the world as an act of worship to the devil. Careful observation of the offer reveals what might be a bit more tempting than you might think. The offer is, "Fall down and worship." The key is in the tense of the words, "fall down and worship."

These verbs are in the aorist tense. This grammatical form of the words indicates an action at a particular point in time. It is not the present tense, which suggests a continuous, ongoing action. In other words, the deal the devil offered Jesus was not to continue to worship the devil. Satan was not saying, I will give you all these kingdoms, but you have to keep on worshiping me. On the contrary, the aorist tense says

> The tension between the Cloud of the Glory of God and the crowd of the glamour of the world is often tilted gradually; one step at a time, one compromise of the text at a time.

Jesus would be given all the kingdoms if He bowed at that point in time, just once. He didn't have to bow down and stay down. He just had to bow "one time," and the devil would give Him the kingdoms.

Let's go a step further. Who was out there in that wilderness, in the desert? In the earth realm, there was only Jesus and the devil. No one else was around. Let's try to read the white spaces in the text. I can imagine the devil looking right, and looking left, saying, "Now, Jesus, there's no one out here but you and me. I won't tell if you won't tell. Nobody will know. Just bow one time. You can get down quickly and get right back up, and I will give you all these kingdoms."

That is often the kind of temptation the devil prepares for us. If he can get us to do it one time, he's got a hold on us. Remember, we got into this sin mess because of one sin. Adam and Eve sinned one time, and mankind was doomed to the innate inclination to sin.

The tension between the Cloud of the Glory of God and the crowd of the glamour of the world is often tilted gradually; one step at a time, one compromise of the text at a time. It starts with one message that diminishes the character, divinity, and holiness of Jesus the Christ. One sacrifice of our integrity comes out of the frustration of seemingly ineffective ministry. One bow often sets us on a path of ungodliness, carnality, and ego-massaging compromise. One bow to the crowd can result in neglect of the cloud of God's glory.

Sometimes God Takes Us on Detours

Being a leader of vision will often take you to the crossroads of choice, often the choice between the glory of God's cloud presence and playing to the crowd. When you choose to go after your God-sized vision, some will go with you, and others will choose not to do so. When God was leading the nation of Israel out of Egyptian bondage, He chose to lead them in unique and powerful ways. This is also the way God chooses to lead us in the twenty-first century. Sometimes the Lord leads us in mysterious ways and sometimes in miraculous ways. Sometimes He leads us in a zigzag line and other times in a straight line. I want you to understand how God leads us.

First, sometimes *the Lord leads us on detours*. The Word of God says that God did not lead them the short way; He led them the long way. He chose not to take them on the shortest route through the wilderness to Canaan. God chose to take them on the long route. Why do you suppose God chose to take them the long way instead of the short way? Well, the Word of God makes it very clear.

God said that if He had led them the short way, they would meet the Philistines, and they would not be ready for war. God knew something about them that they did not know about themselves. Maybe they thought they were ready for the fight of their life, but God knew they weren't ready for it yet. So God took them the long way. It was one thing for the Lord to bring them out of Egypt. It was another thing to get Egypt out of them. In fact, it took Him a lot longer to get Egypt out of them than it was to bring them out of Egypt. So God led them on a detour.

Sometimes God leads you on a detour to teach you how to walk. He slows things down. He puts things in your path that you did not see coming. Have you ever been driving on a trip or going through a city, and all of a sudden you see a detour sign? Well, your GPS didn't tell you there was a detour ahead, but all of a sudden you realize it's going to take you longer than you thought it was going to take. That's what detours do. Detours teach you how to walk. Detours teach you how to handle delays.

But God does not leave you alone when He leads you on the detour. What did He do for the nation of Israel? He had a cloud in the day and a pillar of fire at night. All they had to do was keep their eyes on the cloud or keep their eyes on the pillar of fire and they would know a sense of timing and the direction to go.

We need to remember that the word "baptism" has two senses. One refers to the application of water as a religious rite, in whatever mode it is done; and the other refers to the sense of dedicating, consecrating, initiating into, identifying with, or bringing under obligation to. It is evidently in this latter sense that the word is used here, denoting that they were devoted to Moses as a leader, they were brought under his laws, they became bound to obey him, and they were placed under his protection and guidance by the miraculous interposition of God. This was done by the fact that their passing through the sea, and under the cloud, following the pillar of fire, in this manner, brought them under the authority and direction of Moses

> Sometimes God leads you on a detour to teach you how to walk. He slows things down. He puts things in your path that you did not see coming.

121

as a leader. It was a public recognition of their being his followers and being bound to obey his laws.

Can you imagine the scene with us? Maybe you're tucking your children into bed and all of a sudden, a man opens a tent and says, "It's not time for bed. It's time to get up and get moving."

You may answer with, "No, we'll do something tomorrow."

The man responds, "But the pillar of fire is moving."

So you pack up your children and belongings and start following the pillar of fire. Maybe you're having breakfast in the morning, and you've just finished giving praise to Jehovah for a new day, when all of a sudden, the clouds begin to move. When God gives you a sign, He gives you a sense of timing and a sense of direction. You don't always have to know where God is going; you simply must be following Him every day.

When we were children in school, just like you, there came a time when we had to learn how to play "follow the leader." We students got in a line and followed the teacher. We didn't know everything there was about the teacher. We didn't even know where the teacher was going, but we followed. When our teacher moved, we moved, and when the teacher stopped, we stopped. We learned how to play follow the leader.

In the past twenty to twenty-five years, much has been written about leadership, but not that much written about "followership." We highly recommend that the most comprehensive treatment of the topic of followership was written by our friend and brother, Dr. Leonard Sweet: *I Am a Follower: The Way, Truth, and Life of Following Jesus*. The last time I checked, the Lord is still the leader, and we're still the followers. Often, we talk about our leadership more than we talk about our followership. The apostle Paul would say, "Follow me as I follow Christ." He wouldn't simply say, "Follow me, and I'll show you the way." It is time for you (and for me and the church in the twenty-first century) to learn how to follow the Lord.

When the Lord puts us on a detour, He teaches us dependence. He teaches us how to move when He moves and to stop when He stops. These are the lessons of the detour. It's so interesting when you think about it because God led the nation of Israel into Egypt. God gave them a promise that one day He would bring them out, but it would be four hundred years before this process would take place. It was a constant detour to ultimately fulfill the promises that God had made to them in a previous generation.

When you choose to go after your God-given vision and follow the path of leadership baptism, you need to understand there are going to be challenges that you didn't antic-

> **When you choose to go after your God-given vision and follow the path of leadership baptism, you need to understand there are going to be challenges that you didn't anticipate.**

ipate. There are going to be problems you didn't think about. There are going to be people who will try to tear you down or discourage you. You won't be able to plan for them. There will be financial challenges you could not calculate because you are on a path you have not been on before.

It is like driving a car in the night fog. All you can see is the dotted line in front of you. But if you keep your eye on the dotted line and you have a sense of direction, you will ultimately end up at the right place. I'm not recommending that you spend your life driving through the fog, but you need to realize that when you decide you are going to do something that has not been done before, the path will not be carved out for you. Therefore, you have to learn to depend on the Lord to lead you in the daytime and to lead you in the nighttime, to lead you in mysterious ways and to lead you in miraculous ways.

Sometimes God Leads Us to Dead Ends

If you don't enjoy the detours, secondly, you're not going to enjoy *the dead ends*. It's one thing for the Lord to lead us on a detour, where life slows down and things get delayed from time to time. But it's another thing for the Lord to intentionally lead us to a dead end. The Bible says in Exodus 14 that God led them to the Red Sea. God did that. They were now hemmed in between the sword and the sea. They couldn't go up and around,

> The phrase "and in the sea" articulates a sense of "baptize."

and they couldn't go down and around because there were mountains above the Red Sea and mountains below the Red Sea. They couldn't go back because Pharaoh and his army were in red-hot pursuit behind them. In fact, they could hear the sound of the chariot wheels. They could hear the sound of the armor, yet they were standing in front of the Red Sea.

It is critical at this point for us to remember that the fathers of Israel were baptized "unto Moses" (εἰς eis). This is the same preposition that is used in the form of baptism prescribed in Matthew 28:19. It means that they were devoted or dedicated to Moses. They received and acknowledged him as their ruler and guide. They professed subjection to his laws and were brought under his authority. They were thus "initiated into" his vision and thus recognized his divine mission and bound them-selves to obey his injunctions.

The whole account in the Old Testament leads us to sup-pose that the cloud either passed before them as a pillar, or that it had the same form in the rear of their camp, or that it was suspended over them and was thus the symbol of the divine protection. It would be altogether improbable that the dark cloud would pervade the camp. It would thus embarrass their movements, and there is not the slightest indication in the Old Testament that it did.

The phrase "and in the sea" articulates a sense of "baptize." The sea referred to here is the Red Sea, and the event was the passage through that sea. The fact in the case was that the Lord caused a strong east wind to blow all night and made the sea dry land, and the waters were divided (Ex. 14:21). The waters were a wall unto them on the right hand and on the left (Ex. 14:22).

From this whole narrative, it is evident that they passed through the sea without being "immersed" in it. The waters were driven into high adjacent walls for the very purpose that they might pass between them dry and safe. The Israelites were in this manner initiated into the vision of Moses, convinced of his divine mission, and brought under subjection to him as their leader, lawgiver, and guide.

It's one thing for the Lord to put us on a detour to teach us how to wait. It's another thing for the Lord to bring us to a dead end to teach us how to walk. And it's another thing for the Lord to bring us to a dead end to teach us how to wait. When the Lord puts us on a detour, He teaches us how to follow through. But when He brings us to dead end, He teaches us how to handle fear.

I want you to see what happened when they got there. Here they are standing at the Red Sea, some two million men and women, and the first thing Moses says is to "fear not." That's almost hilarious to us. God brings them to a fearful place and tells them not to be afraid. God knows something about human nature. We will never overcome fear until we're willing to face it and walk through it.

It's like the person who is afraid to get on an airplane. He goes to the airport and watches the planes take off and land, thinking that's going to help him overcome his fear of flying. He won't ever overcome his fear of flying until he gets on that plane and takes off and lands, probably many different times. With this same fear, the nation of Israel has been brought to the brink of disaster. They are standing on the edge of the Red Sea, and Moses says, "Be not afraid."

When you choose to go after the God-given vision, through leadership baptism, you will face fears from time to time: fear of what other people may think, fear of how you would provide for this, fear of the unknown, fear of questions that no one else has asked. Yet you have to be figuring out an answer, a solution that applies to many, and maybe multitudes, not just to a few.

> When we learn to wait on the Lord and allow Him to fight the fight of faith with us and for us, we will never, ever again see the things that we have dreaded, feared, and fretted over the most.

Not only did Moses say, "Fear not," but then he also said, "Stand still." It's interesting that he told them not to try to solve it, not to try to move, but to stand still. He was teaching them that waiting on God is not wasting time before God. He is also teaching them that if you learn to wait on the Lord He will truly renew your strength. What's interesting about the story is that on this particular evening, the pillar of fire is no longer in front of them; it is behind them. It is God that is protecting His people from Pharaoh and his advancing army. Moses goes on to say that they will never, ever see them again. When we learn to wait on the Lord and allow Him to fight the fight of faith with us and for us, we will never, ever again see the things that we have dreaded, feared, and fretted over the most.

Then Moses tells everybody to be quiet. That is one of the hardest things the nation of Israel could ever do because they liked to talk, murmur, and complain about almost everything. Negativism may spread, but negativism doesn't save. If you want to know what's in a person's heart, just listen to what he or she talks about all the time. Moses was teaching the nation of Israel to be still, to be unafraid, to be quiet, and to wait upon the Lord.

Just because an idea comes to your mind doesn't mean you have to say it. Just because a thought crosses your mind doesn't mean you have to express it. It's powerful to pause before you speak and decide whether it's worthy of even uttering. So many people have a self-fulfilling prophecy because they sit around and talk about how bleak things are, and you know what? Usually things become bleak and bad because they turn out to be a self-fulfilling prophecy. You and I are going in the direction of our most dominating thought. We are going in the direction of what propels us forward according to how we think in our lives.

Moses then picks up the rod of God, waves it across the Red Sea, and of course you know the story. God parts the waters, turns a dead end into a four-lane highway, and nearly two million people walk through on dry ground. What is interesting about the story is that the Bible doesn't tell us about the first ones to get into the water. The Bible doesn't make that clear to us, but there were some who took that first step of faith as those waters were parting, wondering if the waters would capsize back on top of them. However, once they took the first step, the others followed.

As you launch out into the vision God has planned for you, some people will never fully understand the step of faith you took, the sacrifices you made, the position you chose, and the path you followed. All they will enjoy is the parted waters. All they will enjoy is the thing that they can see. But they didn't see what it took for it to become a reality. They didn't see the forty years of the wilderness wandering that Moses did before he announced to Pharaoh that it was time for the people to depart. The Bible says God led them through the Red Sea to the other side, and Pharaoh and his army tried, but, of course, were destroyed. The chariot wheels washed on the seashore of the Red Sea, and archaeologists to this day have found the ancient ruins of Pharaoh and his army from so many centuries ago.

Sometimes God Leads Us To Dry Holes

There are going to be detours and dead ends when you choose to go after what God has for you and the dream that He has put in your heart. You also need to be prepared for the *dry holes*. When they got on the other side of the Red Sea, Moses was their hero. In fact, the first song in the Bible was written in Exodus chapter 15, and then the last song in the Bible is in the book of Revelation. It's called "The Song of the Lamb," but the first song was all about Moses. Moses was their hero; it was the number one song of the land. Everybody was singing it. It was number one on the charts, but three days later, Moses went from hero to zero.

Three days later, nobody was singing the song of Moses. No one was excited ever again to hear the song of Moses. Why? Because they had entered a dry period. They entered a very difficult and fragmented time in their wilderness wanderings. It's one thing for you to learn how to handle the detours and to walk, the dead ends and to wait, but the dry holes in worship are at a totally different level. When people disappoint you, when things seem to be so bad, or people have walked away, how do you handle those moments in your life? Are you going to get larger, or are you going to get smaller? Are you going to become a connector, or are you going to choose to become a complainer? Are you going to become one filled with faith, or are you going to turn around and go back the other way?

The Word of God says that they have run out of water, and now they are looking everywhere, trying to find it. They go to this well, to that well; can you even imagine the disappointment they are experiencing? The disappointment of this dry hole, the disappointment of that dry hole, and the situation has become extremely serious because within a matter of days, you can lose a million people with a lack of water. So the people began to murmur and complain. In fact, it gets so bad that in Exodus 16:8, Moses addresses the people and says, "Your murmurings are not against us but against the Lord."

Whatever is in the well of the heart will come out in the bucket of speech. Just listen to what people like to talk about, and you will know what's in their minds and in their hearts. If you're going to enjoy what God has for you, sooner or later you're going to have to realize that even though you are walking through a dry period, God knows how to provide when other people seemingly have turned away and walked back on their commitment.

Whatever is in the well of the heart will come out in the bucket of speech.

Murmuring Stifles Spiritual Growth

So the children of Israel were murmuring and complaining. Do you know what murmuring does? It stifles spiritual growth. Murmuring digs a rut that becomes a grave. Murmuring is what stops people from moving forward. Have you ever spent time with someone you haven't seen in years who is still complaining about the same thing from five or ten years ago? He says things like, "When Betty behaves, I'm going to grow up," or, "When Bob does right, I will move forward," yet it's not really about Betty or Bob. It's about that person deciding to move forward and move out of what others have chosen to live their lives with.

The Bible says the Israelites are facing a difficult time. They are murmuring, and it was in this situation that God says, "This is enough." He says, "Because of your murmuring I am going to let you die in the wilderness." It was the murmuring that brought them down. It was the complaining to God that ultimately caused them to dig their own graves in the wilderness. Now was this God's plan for their life? No, but God was bringing them through a testing to find out what was inside.

When we get up in the morning, we squeeze the toothpaste tube, and toothpaste comes out. When life squeezes you, what comes out of you? Is it sour, or is it sweet? Is it pleasant, or is it painful? Is it joyful, or is it the most negative, terrible thing you could ever express? What comes out of you is so much the picture of what you become or who you have chosen to become. And it was there that God let them die.

Let us tell you how serious murmuring is. When you look in 1 Corinthians chapter 6, you will find that Paul is writing to the church in Corinth. He says, "Don't be like the Israelites were when they created idols and they worshipped. Don't be like the Israelites were when they tempted God." Then he says, in essence, "Don't be like the Israelites were when they committed immorality or adultery." And then he says, "And don't be like the Israelites were when they murmured." He put murmuring in the same bed with immorality, idolatry, and tempting God. If you want to understand who you are, just look at the people in your life. We attract who we are, not what we want. If you're ever going to fulfill your God-sized dream, you're going to have to spend time with the right people. Choose your friends carefully, and let go of those who choose to live their lives filled with the most negative expressions. You're going to have to move forward in what God has for you.

Sometimes the Water Is Bitter

Then Moses sees a river called Marah, a name that means "bitter." Can you even imagine? The people think they're saved. The people think, "We have found the river. We'll have plenty of water," but when they get there to taste it, it's bitter. Sometimes it's that way. As you're carving your path, as you're going into the unknown, there are things that you will taste and say, "That tastes so bitter to me." Yet the Lord has a way of turning what is bitter into sweet. Moses takes the limb of a tree, throws it into the river, and the Bible says the water becomes sweet. Now they have salvation—the two million people have plenty of water. But they're still going to die in the wilderness because they have chosen to live that way.

> For us to accomplish what God has planned for us, we have to take the cross of Jesus Christ daily, put it into the fountainhead of our heart, and allow the sweetness to come out in a bitter-filled world.

For us to accomplish what God has planned for us, we have to take the cross of Jesus Christ daily, put it into the fountainhead of our heart, and allow the sweetness to come out in a bitter-filled world. Until we learn this and learn how, as the apostle Paul would say, "to die to self daily," we will never achieve what God has for us. These are the detours that teach us how to walk. These are the dead ends that teach us how to wait. These are the dry holes that teach us how to worship.

What's so amazing as this story comes to a close? The Bible says in Exodus 13:17–19 that God gives instructions through Moses for some people to go back in and get the bones of Joseph. The Bible doesn't tell us who they chose to go find the box that contains the bones of Joseph. But they go in, find the box, and bring it out of Egypt, and Joseph goes along with the two million people. While they are burying people in the wilderness, Joseph just continues on the journey. He had said that when they leave, "You have to promise that you'll take me with you." They carry him the entire wilderness time of some forty years. They carry him in Canaan for ten to fifteen more years, and finally they bury him in a small town called Shechem. That's the same place that Joseph buried his dad, Jacob, more than one hundred years earlier. It simply means a place of prosperity. It is here that Joseph is buried, in prosperity.

The point is this: what God starts in your life, He will finish in your life. If you stay faithful, one day you will hold in your hands the vision that God has put in your heart. You'll be able to say that what God whispered to you in the night has become a reality in the daytime. Don't allow individuals around you to rob you of what God has put in your heart. Determine that you're going to pursue it, and stay faithful, and God will provide for you.

We can tell you there have been those times of delay in our ministries. We've had to learn how to walk instead of run. There have been those dead ends where we just did not know what we were going to do next or how we were going to get through a difficulty. There have been dry holes where people have chosen not to follow through, or tried to dismantle or undermine us. But we decided that high ground was better than low ground, that the second mile is better than the first mile, and that we have to pursue and stay faithful until the vision becomes a reality.

We want to encourage you to do the same. Whatever vision God has placed in your heart, pursue it today, and you will see in time that what's in your heart, you will hold in your hand!

Visionary Leader Spotlight: John Wesley

In late 1735, a ship made its way to the New World from England. On board was a young Anglican minister, John

Wesley, who had been invited to serve as a pastor to British colonists in Savannah, Georgia. When the weather went sour, the ship found itself in serious trouble. Wesley, also chaplain of the vessel, feared for his life.

But he noticed that the group of German Moravians, who were on their way to preach to American Indians, were not afraid at all. In fact, throughout the storm, they sang calmly. When the trip ended, he asked the Moravian leader about his serenity, and the Moravian responded with a question: Did he, Wesley, have faith in Christ? Wesley said he did, but later reflected, "I fear they were vain words."[33]

In fact, Wesley was confused by the experience. His perplexity led him to a period of soul searching and finally to one of the most famous and consequential conversions in church history.

Wesley was born into a strong Anglican home: his father, Samuel, was priest, and his mother, Susanna, taught religion and morals faithfully to her nineteen children. Wesley attended Oxford, proved to be a fine scholar, and was soon ordained into the Anglican ministry. At Oxford, he joined a society (founded by his brother, Charles) whose members took vows to lead holy lives, take Communion once a week, pray daily, and visit prisons regularly. In addition, they spent three hours every afternoon studying the Bible and other devotional material.

From this "holy club" (as fellow students mockingly called it), Wesley sailed to Georgia to be a pastor. His experience proved to be a failure. A woman he courted in Savannah married another man. When he tried to enforce the disciplines of the "holy club" on his church, the congregation rebelled. A bitter Wesley returned to England.

After speaking with another Moravian, Peter Boehler, Wesley concluded that he lacked saving faith. Though he

---

[33] "John Wesley." Wikipedia. July 30, 2017.

continued to try to be good, he remained frustrated. "I was indeed fighting continually, but not conquering...I fell and rose, and fell again." On May 24, 1738, he had an experience that changed everything. He described the event in his journal:

> In the evening, I went very unwillingly to a society in Aldersgate Street, where one was reading Luther's preface to the Epistle to the Romans. About a quarter before nine, while he was describing the change which God works in the heart through faith in Christ, I felt my heart strangely warmed. I felt I did trust in Christ, Christ alone for salvation, and an assurance was given me that he had taken away my sins, even mine, and saved me from the law of sin and death.

Meanwhile, another former member of the "holy club," George Whitefield, was having remarkable success as a preacher, especially in the industrial city of Bristol. Hundreds of working-class poor, oppressed by industrializing England and neglected by the church, were experiencing emotional conversions under his fiery preaching. So many were responding that Whitefield desperately needed help.

Wesley accepted Whitefield's plea hesitantly. He distrusted Whitefield's dramatic style, he questioned the propriety of Whitefield's outdoor preaching (a radical innovation for the day), and he felt uncomfortable with the emotional reactions even his own preaching elicited. But the orderly Wesley soon warmed to the new method of ministry.

With his organizational skills, Wesley quickly became the new leader of the movement. But Whitefield was a firm Calvinist, whereas Wesley couldn't swallow the doctrine of predestination. Furthermore, Wesley argued (against

Reformed doctrine) that Christians could enjoy entire sanc-tification in this life: loving God and their neighbors, meek-ness and lowliness of heart, abstaining from all appearance of evil, and doing all for the glory of God. In the end, the two preachers parted ways.

Wesley did not intend to found a new denomination, but historical circumstances and his organizational genius con-spired against his desire to remain in the Church of England. Wesley's followers first met in private home "societies." When these societies became too large for members to care for one another, Wesley organized "classes," each with eleven members and a leader. Classes met weekly to pray, read the Bible, discuss their spiritual lives, and collect money for charity. Men and women met separately, but anyone could become a class leader.

The moral and spiritual fervor of the meetings is expressed in one of Wesley's most famous aphorisms: "Do all the good you can, by all the means you can, in all the ways you can, in all the places you can, at all the times you can, to all the people you can, as long as ever you can." The movement grew rapidly, as did its critics, who called Wesley and his fol-lowers "Methodists," a label they wore proudly. It got worse than name calling at times: Methodists were frequently met with violence as paid ruffians broke up meetings and threat-ened Wesley's life.

Although Wesley scheduled his itinerant preaching so it wouldn't disrupt local Anglican services, the bishop of Bristol still objected. Wesley responded, "The world is my parish"—a phrase that later became a slogan of Methodist mission-aries. Wesley, in fact, never slowed down, and during his ministry he traveled more than four thousand miles annually, preaching some forty thousand sermons in his lifetime.

A few Anglican priests, such as his hymn-writing brother, Charles, joined these Methodists, but the bulk of the preaching burden rested on John. He was eventually forced to employ lay preachers, who were not allowed to serve Communion but merely served to complement the ordained ministry of the Church of England.

Wesley then organized his followers into a "connection" and a number of societies into a "circuit" under the leadership of a "superintendent." Periodic meetings of Methodist clergy and lay preachers eventually evolved into the "annual conference," where those who were to serve each circuit were appointed, usually for three-year terms.

In 1787, Wesley was required to register his lay preachers as non-Anglicans. Meanwhile, on the other side of the Atlantic, the American Revolution isolated Yankee Methodists from their Anglican connections. To support the American movement, Wesley independently ordained two lay preachers and appointed Thomas Coke as superintendent. With these and other actions, Methodism gradually moved out of the Church of England—though Wesley himself remained an Anglican until his death.

An indication of his organizational genius, we know exactly how many followers Wesley had when he died: 294 preachers, 71,668 British members, 19 missionaries (5 in mission stations), and 43,265 American members with 198 preachers. Today Methodists number about 30 million worldwide.[34]

---

[34] "John Wesley." Christianity Today. (www.christianitytoday.com/history/people/denominationalfounder/joh-wesley.html)

CHAPTER 8

THE VISIONARY PORTRAIT

Dr. Elmer Towns is a cofounder of Liberty University in Lynchburg, Virginia, and dean of the Global Church Learning Center (www.GCLC.tv) ,with more than sixty thousand pastors/leaders being trained online. He enjoys teaching "The Visionary Portrait: How to Cast Vision & Mobilize Leaders." Below is a summary of this remarkable teaching on how to paint a vision for your organization and to see your leaders baptized into your God-given vision.

Begin with the Horizon

"First, you must begin with the horizon. With your Spirit-filled imagination, take your mental sketchbook and paint your horizon." What is the horizon? "Before you draw the horizon in, if you draw the horizon down, that means you're going to have a lot of sky, which means you're going to make people think without. If you put your horizon high on the page, that means you're going to look at the Earth a lot and that's going to make people think within. Our vision needs to be more about our God than about us. It has to be about God and what He is doing in the world. Make your visionary portrait about Him, not about you. Where are you going to put your horizon? Put your horizon so it includes God."

Paint in Some Mountains

Second, you have to paint in some mountains. Life is filled with problems. Before you witness your vision becoming victories and your dreams becoming destinies, there will be a lot of mountains to claim, climb, and conquer. "Man born of woman is of many troubles," Job said. He said, "You've got to put mountains; you've got to put barriers there."

Barriers come in all shapes and sizes. Some problems are big. Others will be steep, sharp mountains. Some will have snow on the top, along with huge rocks.

Some problems are small, and you've got rolling mountains out there. Some problems are close, while other problems are going to happen a long time away from now. Thus, when you cast your vision to your people, be sure to highlight the kinds of mountains you anticipate having to climb to see your vision come to pass. Be sure to highlight both the large

> Make your visionary portrait about Him, not about you. Where are you going to put your horizon? Put your horizon so it includes God.

mountains and the small ones. We realize that some mountains are so far away that we cannot even see them yet!

Wherever you put your mountains, wherever you put your problems, give an element of reality to your visionary painting. Without mountains, there is not realism in your vision. We have to deal with problems. If you don't deal with problems in your vision, you are being unrealistic. Your problem can be too small of a building; it can be that you're at the end of town. We don't know what your problems are, but you have to deal with circumstantial problems, personality problems, historic problems, city problems, civic problems, ethical problems, financial problems, and more.

Paint a Visionary Path

Third, we need to paint a visionary path. You need to draw a path from where you are, toward the mountains and out the other side. There are several kinds of paths. You can articulate a big, broad expressway. Yet this really is not the way life is lived. There are delays and challenges on the highway of life.

You can draw a winding path. You can put problems—rocks—in your path. You can paint potholes or water puddles in your path. We challenge you to cast a vision with a path because your painting needs movement. If your visionary leadership doesn't have movement to show action, people are just going to look at it and walk away. The path will determine action.

Add Some Flowers Growing

Fourth, you need to paint some flowers in your vision. We need to place some growing things in our portrait. You want some flowers along the path, and you might put some bushes with the flowers. You might add some trees and bushes that are growing. You should include some trees far away. In life; we need to have them close-up so that our followers can see them and smell them but also see a way out in the future. In other words, as we share the vision, people will be drawn to it if the vision includes growth, hope, faith, and victory.

Include Some Birds Soaring

Next, we need to paint some birds in the visionary portrait. Paint some birds in your sky. Birds detach themselves from this Earth. They make the spirit soar. You can put a whole flock of birds, or you can draw one bird. You can add a big bird or a small bird, but when people see birds, it will cause their spirits to soar when they hear and see your vision. As you prepare to share your God-given vision, when people see the "growing things" and the "soaring things," they will be compelled to want to become involved with the vision. When people buy in to your vision, they buy in to your leadership!

Show People on the Path

Sixth, paint people in the visionary portrait. Be sure to put people on the path. Life is going somewhere. People must be going somewhere. Show them where the visionary path will take them. Also, you can paint children and adults on this path. The people on the

> Life is going somewhere. People must be going somewhere.

path are moving toward the mountains—toward the problems. As a visionary leader, you have already seen the path through the mountains to the other side.

Paint Yourself into the Vision

Last, paint yourself in the visionary picture. Your vision is nothing if it doesn't include you. What is God doing in you, for you, to you, and through you? Share your testimony with your church, organization, or ministry. Bring your people into the inner sanctum of your soul. In your picture, show yourself as a servant leader who is possessed with a God-given vision and is passing it on to his people.[35]

---

[35] Towns, Elmer. "Casting Vision & Mobilizing Leaders", Global Church Learning Center. 2015.

Casting vision is one of the most sacred and strategic assignments that a leader has the privilege to communicate to his or her church, organization, or ministry. Also, there are times and instances when the visionary leader has the opportunity to cast a large enough vision to encompass many organizations at once. It is critical for the servant leader to articulate this vision correctly because often, he or she gets only once chance at it.

We love getting into the challenge of discerning the Lord's will as we work through the process with others. We learned some years ago that the bigger the vision, the more important it is that you involve people from all walks of life, even in carving the final vision. Once that vision is done and written up specifically, the biggest challenge is communicating it effectively. When we are casting our vision, we need to filter it by ensuring that the vision can be described in the following ways.

Clear

Ronnie Floyd, Senior Pastor of Cross Church of Springdale, Arkansas states, "Clarity around a vision is imperative. As the communicator, you must be clear about your understanding of it before sharing it with others. Therefore, writing the vision is also extremely important."[36] It has been said, "Over the lips and through the fingertips brings clarity to the speaker and to his or her listeners." Pastor Floyd continues, "This well-written documentation is what you will return to again and again. Through a meticulous process, you learn how to communicate the vision with exactitude. When the vision is clear to you, you are more able to clearly communicate it to others."[37]

---

[36] Floyd, Ronnie. The 4 C's of Effective Vision Casting. Pastors.com. November 1, 2013.

[37] Towns, Elmer. "Casting Vision & Mobilizing Leaders", Global Church Learning Center. 2015.

Whether you are communicating the vision of the church or the vision for a new initiative, ensure that you do so with absolute clarity. It is not about how much you share, but you must share enough for people to have complete clarity. When people walk away from hearing the vision for the first time, instead of them saying, "Why?" you want them to walk away saying, "Wow!" Therefore, when you cast vision to God's people, be sure it is clear.

Concrete

Pastor Floyd says, "We think having a concrete vision means you have a vision that is real and tangible. It is not about using language no one understands or trying to impress others with great and extensive content. It is a vision that people can touch, feel, and become engaged in personally."[38]

> When people walk away from hearing the vision for the first time, instead of them saying, "Why?" you want them to walk away saying, "Wow!"

There are times when Christian leaders seem to spiritualize a lot of issues when they cast vision. Yet the late Dr. Adrian Rogers used to say, "You cannot manage spiritual things, and you can spiritualize management things."[39] In other words, two plus two equals four, whether you are in the ministry world or the business world. We cannot always spiritualize an initiative and have it received by the people. We have to know God wants us to do it, even have it confirmed from His Word. Yet we have to communicate the vision in a believable and

---

[38] Towns, Elmer. "Casting Vision & Mobilizing Leaders", Global Church Learning Center. 2015.

[39] Rogers, Adrian. Beyond All Limits Conference. January, 2002.

tangible manner. A balanced vision talks about the happy by and by and the nasty now and now!

Concise

Powerful communicators have learned to make every word count. In today's world, it is really true: less is more. This is especially true when we cast a vision. It needs to be concise. It needs to be brief, broad, big, and believable.

We are called to deliver a God-sized vision in bite-sized pieces. It is important for it to be large enough to move the souls of people. Yet it needs to be small enough so people can see themselves in the vision. Yes, you have to go deep and comprehend the details so you know you understand the vision. Yet when you cast it before others, they just need to know the work is already done.

> As a servant-leader, you are God's instrument to rally the people to a better future.

You need to be on top of it, but remember, you are breaking it down—not only so others can grasp it, but also for them to be able to communicate it to others. We will state it again: it is not about how much you share; share enough for the people to have complete clarity.

Compelling

Pastor Ronnie Floyd wraps it up by stating:

> A compelling vision moves the people to action. As a servant-leader, you are God's instrument to rally the people to a better future. You are there to lead them into a future where they would not go on their own. The vision must

be clear enough for them to understand, concrete enough for them to believe it is real, concise enough for them to communicate, and compelling enough for them to own personally and enthusiastically.

As the communicator of the vision, do your very best to be strong, believable, and capable of moving people into owning the vision enthusiastically. If the vision is going to capture their imaginations and hearts, moving them into the vision personally and enthusiastically, then the vision must be compelling.[40]

When we are casting vision, we desire for people to say, "Yes! Count me in!" The late Dr. Bill Bright, the founder of Campus Crusade for Christ, used to say, "Small dreams never inflame the hearts of big people." If you wish for big people to join you, then you must learn how to cast a large enough vision to grab the attention of people from all walks of life.

Visionary Leader Spotlight: George Washington

Why did George Washington emerge as the most significant leader in the founding of the United States of America, even to the extent of being called the Father of the Country?

At the three major junctions in the founding of the nation—the revolution, the Constitutional Convention, and election of the first president—for each position, the leader chosen was George Washington. In his own day, he was seen as the indispensable man, the American Moses, The Father of the Country. Why?

---

[40] Floyd, Ronnie. The 4 C's of Effective Vision Casting. Pastors.com. November 1, 2013.

His contemporaries and subsequent commentators have enumerated many factors that caused his peers to select him for these three strategically important positions. The most commonly cited characteristic given for his emergence as the supreme leader is his character.

We want to suggest and argue that Washington was chosen for these leadership roles because of his character and also because of his being a genius in the area of leadership. People trusted him because he had demonstrated a noble and incorruptible character. He had also shown himself to be an exceptional leader.

Many American historians consider Richard Stazesky's work entitled, "George Washington, Genius in Leadership"[41] to be among some of the best concepts relating to this revolutionary leader.

The visionary leader, first of all, has very clear, encompassing, and far-reaching vision with regard to the cause or organization involved. This vision includes ideas and goals that remain constant, no matter how long it takes to realize them and regardless of the difficulties the leader encounters. Furthermore, the leader never allows any of the means or actions along the way to violate or invalidate this vision and its constituent values.

Second, the visionary leader is skillful in designing and creating an organizational culture that will make possible the attainment of the leader's vision and ideas. In fact, creating this organizational culture may be the most lasting contribution of the leader because it will consist of the enduring values, vision, and beliefs that members of the organization share.

Third, the visionary leader is also a person who can attract others to follow him or her in seeking attainment of

---

[41] Stazesky, Richard C. "George Washington, Genius in Leadership," *The Washington Papers*. February 22, 2000.

145

the vision. But more than that, this charismatic person is able to instill in others the ideas, beliefs, and values of the vision so that they become empowered to move beyond the leader's and their own expectations.

In brief, the visionary leader has a vision into the far future, can develop an effective organization, and can attract others to strive also for the attainment of his or her vision so that it becomes a shared vision. They all work together in an organization that sustains the vision, its beliefs, and its values.

Another characteristic of a truly effective leader is that she or he always focuses simultaneously on two seemingly different configurations. For example, visionary leaders always need to combine strategy and tactics, goals and objectives, big-picture ideas

> Another characteristic of a truly effective leader is that she or he always focuses simultaneously on two seemingly different configurations.

and little-picture details, architect and plumber, wisdom and application, profound and practical, complex and simple, futuristic ideas and present actions.

Of all the founding fathers, George Washington alone demonstrated fully the threefold characteristics of a visionary leader and the intellectual and moral capacity, over a long period of time and in the course of manifold difficulties, to maintain coherency between long-range ideas and goals and short-term actions.

On June 15, 1775, the delegates to the Continental Congress, meeting in Philadelphia, unanimously elected George Washington to command all the continental forces, raised, or to be raised for the defense of American liberty. His commission, dated June 19, 1775, designated him general and commander in chief of the United Colonies. He received it on the twentieth, and he started for Boston on the twenty-first.[42]

Consider first his role as a visionary leader. He envisioned this nation as contributing to the uplifting and happiness of the whole world in the years, even centuries, to come.

As a visionary leader, Washington developed an organization with an organizational culture that achieved the goal of winning the war for independence. This, as Washington well knew, would be just the first step in the founding of a republican, constitutional government.

As a visionary leader, Washington also attracted both military and civilians to follow him to victory. He faced the realities of short-term enlistments, desertions, very poorly clad and equipped soldiers, recalcitrant congressional and state legislators, and wavering loyalty to the Glorious Cause among the populace. Yet enough soldiers and civilians so trusted him, believed in him, and loved him that they stayed with him and his ideas.

Washington excelled in all three roles of a visionary leader; he excelled equally in maintaining coherence between his long-term goals and specific, current actions. As the general and commander in chief, George Washington became America's true hero and, to use our terms, America's visionary role model because of his exemplary character revealed with his unparalleled visionary leadership and his ability to maintain coherence between his far-reaching ideas and his immediate words and actions.

As the unanimously elected presiding officer of the Constitutional Convention, which met in Philadelphia from May 25 to September 17, 1787, Washington again demonstrated his genius in leadership. In terms of leadership of the convention, he was equally effective as a visionary leader and a long-range/short-range thinker. His style, however, changed, for he

---

[42] "George Washington." Wikipedia. June, 10, 2017.

was a presiding officer, not a general. It was a very well-organized convention. All sessions were held in secrecy, with no disclosures of the proceedings revealed to anyone else.

The success of the convention, both in terms of its process and outcome, testify to the genius of Washington's visionary leadership, just as its final confirmation by the American people did. Historians and commentators of that day and subsequent years credit Washington's and also Franklin's endorsements for bringing about the ratification of the Constitution to be the law of the land.

It was no surprise to anyone in the nation, including George Washington, that he was unanimously elected as the first president of the new nation and that four years later he was reelected to this preeminent position. Just as with his other calls to duty by the people, Washington was chosen not only on the basis of his character and leadership skills but also because the people knew and trusted his ideas and commitments.

> The success of the convention, both in terms of its process and outcome, testify to the genius of Washington's visionary leadership, just as its final confirmation by the American people did.

Evaluating him as the first president in terms of the visionary leader, it is clear that Washington had a very well-developed and coherent vision with both long- and short-range goals. Some of these ideas were the absolute necessity and even sacredness of the Union; faithful obedience to the Constitution; development of a distinctly American national character; establishment of a government that would be trusted by the people; the role of the federal government in the furtherance of industry, commerce, education, and what today we call infrastructure; the need in a republic for public and private virtue; independence from all forms of foreign dominance; and the maintenance of liberty.

Washington was responsible for the creation of a federal government. He did so, and we live today with and by much of what he created. He demonstrated his skill as an organizational leader as a strict constitutionalist and by his belief that Congress was primarily responsible for the creation of domestic policies and laws, while the president was responsible for carrying out the policies and enforcing the laws.[43]

[43] Stazesky, Richard C. "George Washington, Genius in Leadership," *The Washington Papers*. February 22, 2000.

CONCLUSION

In 2006, I (James O. Davis) made a trip to Lisbon, Portugal. While I was in Lisbon, I arranged for a driver to take me to Palos, Spain. To get to Palos, Spain, one has to really want to go there. There is no direct route, but the trip is worth taking to go to one of the greatest historic places in the world. For many years, I'd wanted to make the trip to Palos, and had never met anyone in the United States or in my association of friends who had ever

> As I stepped into this room, I was stepping back more than five hundred years. This room was just as it was in 1491.

been there. I got up early in the morning and left at 5:00 a.m. from Lisbon so I could arrive by 9:00 a.m. at a monastery in Palos. If you ever get the opportunity to go to Palos, I encourage you to do so. I believe it is one of the greatest trips a visionary leader could ever take in his or her life.

I roamed around in the monastery looking at the artifacts. It was a gorgeous summer day. After I had looked at a lot of the artifacts, I walked into a very small room, measuring probably six feet by eight feet. It is what I call "the vision room." On the top of the doorpost was a plaque that said these words "The Birthplace of America." I had always thought the birthplace of America was in Plymouth, Massachusetts, where the Pilgrims had landed in the 1400s. But no, this plaque said this room was the birthplace of America!

As I stepped into this room, I was stepping back more than five hundred years. This room was just as it was in 1491.

There were two chairs opposite each other with a table between them. Above the chair on the right was a picture of Christopher Columbus. I sat in the same chair that Columbus would have sat in 1491. And while I sat in that chair, I looked across that small room at the other empty chair, where a Franciscan monk would have sat when Columbus shared his vision for the new world. The vision he had was to stop going around the tip of Africa and to make his way across the Atlantic Ocean. The belief was this new trade route would lead them to India. He shared his vision of the new trade routes, his vision of the new world, and it was there that the Franciscan monk caught the vision. He then took it to the queen and king of Spain, who both decided that their nation would fund the vision of Christopher Columbus.

What's so ironic is that Christopher Columbus was born in Italy, he was raised in Portugal, and he'd already taken the same vision to the Portuguese leaders, but they laughed at him. They did not believe in the vision, much less the visionary. So, Christopher Columbus went next door to the neighbors, and they bought into the vision. And as you know, that vision changed the world, changed the course of human history. We are outcomes of that vision. To this day, I've often wondered if the Portuguese leaders could have the chance to do it all over again, if they would have changed their minds and funded the vision, the mission, of Christopher Columbus. I wonder what our world would be like today. I wonder if we would speak English or if we would even speak Portuguese.

When I left that venue, a driver took me to a very old Catholic Church. It sat on the edge of a rock wall where the Atlantic Ocean used to bank up against it, centuries ago. I knocked on the door of the Catholic Church. The priest was not there. A woman who worked at the Catholic Church was there; she spoke no English. The driver spoke Spanish, so they were able to communicate. I said to her, "I'd like to go inside."

She said, "Sorry, cannot do that. The priest is not here."
I said to her again, "Please, I ask you, let me go inside."
She said, "Sorry, the priest is not here."

She did not realize that sometimes I make coffee nervous. And with my tenacity, I said, "Please, call the priest. Tell him that an American leader has come, and he would just love to have five minutes or so inside the Catholic Church."

She called the priest, came back, and welcomed me in. I was grateful to have the opportunity to go in this beautiful, ancient Catholic Church. Immediately, I went down front, and it was at that altar that Christopher Columbus dedicated his men and his mission to God. He dedicated his cause to Jesus Christ. I pondered the reality of this man who was able to articulate what his cause was and what his vision was and able to mobilize a group of men who would, ultimately, help change the world.

Months later, after the first expedition to the New World, Christopher Columbus would come back to the same church, and to that same altar, and give praise and glory to God for all that he'd seen and all that he'd been able to accomplish.

While I was there on the premises, I went outside and walked to a beautiful grassy lawn. It is the same place where, more than five hundred years ago, Christopher Columbus and his men would have gotten on three simple, small boats, cross the Atlantic Ocean, and make their way to the New World. As I walked on that lush, grassy lawn, I knelt by a rushing fountain and asked the Lord for big things. I asked the Lord to help us fulfill the Great Commission. I prayed that the Lord would double the size of the church and would make it harder for someone to die without hearing the glorious Gospel of Jesus Christ.

God has entrusted you with "his vision" for your life and for your church or organization. This is your moment. It is your opportunity to help shape the future of your generation.

As a fellow leader, I (Kenneth Ulmer) challenge you to remember: leaders lead by vision. God never "wastes" vision. He trusts you with the vision that brings Him glory. In fact, He takes a risk when He gives us vision. He takes a risk that we will deny the vision and refuse to walk in the revelation He gives us. Sometimes because of sin. Sometimes because of fear. Sometimes because of discouragement. He gives vision and takes a risk that we will deny it. He takes a risk that we will distort it and use it for our own aggrandizement. He takes a risk that we will use it to abuse those precious ones He sends to follow the vision.

> **God has entrusted you with "his vision" for your life and for your church or organization. This is your moment. It is your opportunity to help shape the future of your generation.**

He takes a risk that we will taint the vision and walk in the weakness and frailty of our sinful desires rather than walking in the Spirit, being filled and led by His spirit. He takes a risk that we will twist the vision for our own selfish desires and lord it, or carnally rule over others, saying, "Thus saith the Lord" when, in fact, the Lord has said no such thing and it is, in fact, "Thus saith I." He risks that we will make our words His words.

Such is the reason He accompanies every vision with an anointing to fulfill that vision. Guard your anointing. Share your vision. Never give it away. God will hold you accountable for the stewardship of the vision He gives you.

May you be blessed as you walk in all God has called you to. May you stand before Him one day and hear Him say, "Well done, thou good and faithful servant." But in the meantime, may He go before you to lead you, beside you to protect you, behind you to push and encourage you, above you to cover you, beneath you to sustain you, and in you to fill you with His presence and His power so that your life of vision stewardship and leadership baptism might bring honor to Him. Amen.

THE FORGOTTEN BAPTISM

ABOUT THE AUTHORS

Bishop Kenneth C. Ulmer, DMin, PhD

Kenneth C. Ulmer, DMin, PhD, is the Senior Pastor of Faithful Central Bible Church in Los Angeles. In 2000, the congregation purchased The Great Western Forum (previous home of the Los Angeles Lakers professional basketball team) which they also operated as a commercial entertainment venue before selling it to Madison Square Garden in 2013.

Dr. Ulmer is a former president of The King's University in Dallas, Texas, where he also serves as a founding board member, adjunct professor, and Director of The King's at Oxford; an annual summer session held at Oxford University.

Dr. Ulmer earned his bachelor of arts degree in broadcasting and music from the University of Illinois. After accepting his call to the ministry, Dr. Ulmer founded Macedonia Bible Baptist Church in San Pedro, California. He has studied at Pepperdine University, Hebrew Union College, the University of Judaism, Christ Church, and Wadham College at Oxford University in England. He earned a PhD from Grace Graduate School of Theology in Long Beach, California, was awarded an Honorary Doctor of Divinity from Southern California School of Ministry, and earned his Doctor of Ministry from United Theological Seminary.

He participated in the study of Ecumenical Liturgy and Worship at Magdalene College at Oxford University in England, has served as instructor in Pastoral Ministry and Homiletic at Grace Theological Seminary, as an adjunct professor at Biola University (where he served on the Board of Trustees) and as an adjunct professor at Pepperdine University. He served as a mentor in the Doctor of Ministry degree program at United Theological Seminary in Dayton, Ohio. Dr. Ulmer was consecrated Bishop of Christian Education of the Full Gospel Baptist Church Fellowship, where he served as a founding member on the Bishops Council. He has served on the Board of Directors of The Gospel Music Workshop of America.

Dr. Ulmer is currently the Presiding Bishop over Macedonia International Bible Fellowship based in Johannesburg, South Africa, which is an association of pastors and church leaders representing ministries in Africa and the United States.

Dr. Ulmer has written several books, including *A New Thing* (a reflection on the Full Gospel Baptist Movement), *Spiritually Fit to Run the Race* (a guide to godly living), *In His Image: An Intimate Reflection of God* (an update of his book *The Anatomy of God*), *Making your Money Count: Why We Have It – How To Manage It* (featured on *This is Your Day* with Benny Hinn), *The Champion in You: Step Into God's Purpose for Your Life*, and *The Power of Money: How to Avoid a Devil's Snare*, *Knowing God's Voice*, and *Passionate God*.

Dr. Ulmer and his wife, Togetta, are residents of Los Angeles, California, and have been married for forty years. They have two daughters, one son, and five granddaughters.

James O. Davis, DMin

Dr. James O. Davis is the founder of Cutting Edge International. He also is a cofounder of Billion Soul Network, a growing coalition of more than 2,400 Christian ministries and denominations synergizing their efforts together to build the premier community of pastors worldwide to help plant five million new churches for a billion-soul harvest. The Billion Soul Network, consisting of 500,000 churches, is the largest pastor network in the world.

Many Christian leaders recognize Dr. Davis as one of the leading networkers in the Christian world. The *Christian Telegraph*, one of the largest Internet portals, named Dr. Davis in its "Top Ten Christian Influencers in the World for 2010" and as "Leader of the Year." His leadership includes the following roles:

- He hosts a biannual Synergize! Pastors' Conference and regional Synergize! Leadership Summits and deployed Billion Soul Leadership Summits in all major world regions. During international summits from 2007 through 2011, leaders committed to plant 5.5 million new churches.
- He leads an annual North American Conference on Biblical Preaching
- More than 80,000 pastors have attended these conferences and summits.
- Before launching the Billion Soul Network, Dr. Davis served for twelve years as the National Evangelists' Representative for the National Assemblies of God world headquarters, where he provided leadership

for some 1,500 evangelists and equipped thousands of students for full-time evangelism.

- He ministers more than forty-five weeks per year to an average yearly audience of more than 150,000 people. In the past thirty years, Dr. Davis has ministered face-to-face to more than ten million people in more than 123 nations.
- Each year, he travels more than 250,000 miles with a combined total of nine million miles.

Dr. Davis earned his doctorate degree in ministry at Trinity Evangelical Divinity School. He earned his bachelor's degree in Bible studies from Central Bible College and earned two master's degrees at the Assemblies of God Theological Seminary.

He is the author or editor of twenty books, including *We Are The Church* with Dr. Leonard Sweet, *The Pastor's Best Friend: The New Testament Evangelist*, *Living Like Jesus*, *The Preacher's Summit: Reaching Your Maximum Potential*, *Gutenberg to Google: The Twenty Indispensable Laws of Communication*, *How to Make Your Net Work: Tying Relational Knots for Global Impact*, *Beyond All Limits: The Synergistic Church for a Planet in Crisis* (cowritten with Dr. Bill Bright), and articles for *Charisma*, *Ministry Today*, *The New York Times Magazine*, and numerous other publications.

Dr. Davis resides in Orlando with his wife, Sheri, and their daughters, Olivia and Priscilla. They also have two children, Jennifer and James, who reside in heaven.

BIBLIOGRAPHY

"Adoniram Judson, First Missionary from the United States." http://www.christianity.com/church/church-history/church-history-for-kids/adoniram-judson-first-missionary-from-the-united-states-11635044.html.

Anderson, James D., and Ezra Earl Jones. *The Management of Ministry: Leadership, Purpose, Structure, Community.* San Francisco; Harper and Row Publishers, 1992.

Axelrod, Alan. *Profiles in Leadership.* New York: Prentice Hall Press, 2003.

Barna, George. *The Power of Vision.* Regal Books, 2009.

Bennis, Warren. *On Becoming a Leader.* Cambridge, MA: Perseus Books Group, 2003.

Bennis, Warren, and Burt Nanus. *Leaders: The Strategies for Taking Charge.* New York: Harper & Row Publishers, 1985.

Bennis, Warren, and Joan Goldsmith. *Learning to Lead: A Workbook on Becoming a Leader*, an updated edition. Cambridge MA: Perseus Books, 1997.

Benowitz, Ellen A. Cliffs Notes. *Quick Review: Principles of Management.* New York: Hungry Minds, 2001.

Blackaby, Henry and Richard Blackaby. *Spiritual Leadership: Moving People on to God's Agenda*. Nashville: Broadman and Holman, 2001.

Blake, Robert R., and Anne Adams McCanse. *Leadership Dilemmas—Grid Solutions*. Austin, TX: Gulf Publishing Company, 1991.

Blanchard, Ken. *The Heart of a Leader: Insights on the Art of Influence*. Tulsa, OK: Honor Books, 1999.

Blanchard, Kenneth H., and Phil Hodges. *The Servant Leader: Transforming Your Heart, Head, Hands, & Habits*. Nashville: J. Countryman, 2003.

Blanchard, Ken, Bill Hybels, and Phil Hodges. *Leadership by the Book: Tools to Transform Your Workplace*. New York: William Morrow & Co., 1999.

Blanchard, Ken, and Spenser Johnson. *The One Minute Manager*. New York: Berkley Publishing, 1982. (A short story with three one-minute secrets: goals, praisings, and reprimands.)

Blanchard, Ken, and Paul Hersey. *Management of Organizational Behavior*. Englewood Cliffs, NJ: Prentice-Hall Inc., 1982. (A major work on contingency and situational leadership within family systems.)

Blank, Warren. *The 108 Skills of Natural-Born Leaders*. New York: Amacom, 2001.

Boice. J. M. *The Sermon on The Mount: An Expositional Commentary*. Wheaton: Crossway Books. 2002.

Briner, Bob. *The Management Methods of Jesus*. Nashville: Broadman and Holman, 1998.

Briner, Bob, and Ray Pritchard. *More Leadership Lessons of Jesus*. Nashville: Broadman & Holman, 1998.

Brown, Patricia D. *Learning to Lead from Your Spiritual Center*. Nashville: Abingdon Press, 1996.

Browning, D., and Leadership Network (Dallas, TX). *Hybrid Church: The Fusion of Intimacy and Impact*. San Francisco, CA: Jossey-Bass Publishers, 2010

Bruce, F. F. *First Corinthians*. Zondervan. 1971.

Bugbee, B. L., and Charles E. Fuller Institute of Evangelism and Church Growth. (1989).

Campbell, Barry. *Toolbox for [Busy] Pastors*. Nashville: Convention Press, 1998.

Carr, Clay. *The New Manager's Survival Manual: All the Skills You Need for Success*. New York: John Wiley & Sons, 1995.

Castells, M. *Communication Power*. Oxford: Oxford University Press, 2009.

Cooper, Robert K., and Ayman Sawaf. *Executive EQ: Emotional Intelligence in Leadership and Organizations*. New York: The Berkley Publishing Group, 1996.

Covey, Stephen R. *The 7 Habits of Highly Effective People: Restoring the Character Ethic*. New York: Fireside/Simon & Schuster, 1990.

Covey, Stephen R. *Principle-Centered Leadership*. New York: Simon and Schuster, 1992. (This is one resource that helped shape the SkillTrack® on Mission-Centered Leadership.)

Daft, Richard L. *The Leadership Experience*. Orlando, FL: Harcourt College Publishers, 2002. (An excellent, useful college text on concepts and practices of leadership.)

Dale, Robert D. *Pastoral Leadership*. Nashville: Abingdon Press, 1986. (Written by a scholar and practitioner, it is biblical, practical, and insightful.)

Davis, James O. *Scaling Your Everest: Lessons Learned from Sir Edmund Hillary*. Orlando: Billion Soul Publishing, 2014.

DePree, Max. *Called to Serve*. Grand Rapids, MI: Eerdmans Publishing, 2001.

DePree, Max. *Leadership Is an Art*, second ed. New York: Currency, 2004.

DePree, Max. *Leadership Jazz*. New York: Dell Publishing, 1992.

Desatnick, Robert L. *Managing to Keep the Customer: How to Achieve and Maintain Superior Customer Service throughout the Organization*. San Francisco: Jossey-Bass Publishers, 1987.

Eigen, Lewis D. *The Manager's Book of Quotations*. New York: Amacon Press, 1991.

Elder, Lloyd. *Blueprints: 10 Challenges for a Great People*. Nashville: Broadman Press, 1984.

"English Bible History." http://www.greatsite.com/timeline-en-glish-bible-history/martin-luther.html.

Falwell, Jerry L. "Vision: Artistic Message." Beyond All Limits Conference. Orlando, 2004.

Ferguson, Rick E. *The Servant Principle: Finding Fulfillment through Obedience to Christ*. Nashville: Broadman & Holman Publishers, 1999.

Ford, Leighton. *Transforming Leadership: Jesus's Way of Creating Vision, Shaping Values, and Empowering Change*. Downers Grove, IL: InterVarsity Press, 1991.

Fraker, Anne T., and Larry C. Spears. *Seeker and Servant: The Private Writings of Robert K. Greenleaf*. San Francisco: Jossey-Bass Publishers, 1996.

Francis, David. *Spiritual Gifts*. Nashville: LifeWay Press, 2003.

Gardner, John W. *On Leadership*. New York: The Free Press, 1990.

George, Carl F., and Robert E. Logan. *Leading and Managing Your Church*. Grand Rapids, MI: Fleming H. Revell, 1987.

Goetz, David L, ed. *Building Church Leaders*. Carol Stream, IL: Leadership Resources *Christianity Today*, 2000. (A loose-leaf binder of training resources.)

Goleman, Daniel. *Working with Emotional Intelligence*. New York: Bantam Books, 2000.

Goleman, Daniel, Richard Boyatzis, and Annie McKee. *Primal Leadership: Learning to Lead with Emotional Intelligence*. Boston: Harvard Business School Publishing, 2002.

Graves, Stephen, and Thomas Addington. *A Case for Calling: Authentic Living in the Workplace*. Nashville: Broadman & Holman Publishers, 1998.

Graves, Stephen, and Thomas Addington. *A Case for Character: Authentic Living in Your Workplace*. Nashville: Broadman & Holman Publishers, 1998.

Graves, Stephen, and Thomas Addington. *A Case for Serving: Responding Selflessly to the Needs of Others*. Nashville: Broadman & Holman Publishers, 1998.

Greenleaf, Robert K. *Servant Leadership: A Journey into the Nature of Legitimate Power and Greatness*. New York: Paulist Press, 1977.

Greenleaf, Robert K. *The Power of Servant-Leadership*. San Francisco: Berrett-Koehler Publishers, Inc., 1998.

Greenleaf, Robert K. *On Becoming a Servant Leader: The Private Writings of Robert K. Greenleaf*. Don T. Frick and Larry C. Spears, eds. San Francisco: Jossey-Bass Publishers, Inc., 1996.

Grenz, Arlo. *The Confident Leader: Getting a Good Start as a Christian Minister*. Nashville: Broadman & Holman, 1994.

Heller, Robert, and Adele Hayward. *Managing for Excellence*. New York: DK Books, 2001.

Herrington, Jim. *The Leader's Journey*. San Francisco: A Leadership Network Publication, 2003.

Hesselbein, Frances. *Hesselbein on Leadership*. New York: Jossey-Bass Publishers, 2002.

Hitt, William D. *Thoughts on Leadership: A Treasury of Quotations*. Columbus, OH: Battelle Press, 1992.

House, Robert J. *Path–Goal Theory of Leadership* (Quoted in *The Leadership Experience* by Richard Daft, see pp.89–91).

Hughes, R. K. *The Sermon on the Mount: The Message of the Kingdom*. Crossway Books, 1981.

Hughes, Selwyn. *Christ-Empowered Living*. Nashville: Broadman & Holman Publishers, 2001.

Hunter, James C. *The Servant: A Simple Story about the True Essence of Leadership*. Roseville, CA: Prima Publishing, 1998.

Hybels, Bill. *Courageous Leadership*. Grand Rapids, MI: Zondervan, 2002.

Jones, Laurie Beth. *Jesus, CEO: Using Ancient Wisdom for Visionary Leadership*. New York: Hyperion Books, 1995.

Jones, Laurie Beth. *Teach Your Team to Fish: Using Ancient Wisdom for Inspired Teamwork*. New York: Three Rivers Press. 2002.

Jones, Gareth R., and Jennifer M. George. *Contemporary Management*, third ed. New York: McGraw-Hill Companies, 2003.

Kinicki, Angelo, and Robert Kreitner. *Organizational Behavior: Key Concepts, Skills, and Best Practices*. New York: McGraw-Hill Publications, 2003.

Kotter, John P. "John P. Kotter on What Leaders Really Do." Cambridge: *Harvard Business Review*, 1999.

Kouzes, James M., and Barry Z. Posner. *The Leadership Challenge: How to Get Extraordinary Things Done in Organizations*. San Francisco: Jossey-Bass Publishers, 1987.

Jackson, J., and J. C. Maxwell. *Pastorpreneur: Pastors and Entrepreneurs Answer the Call*. Friendswood, TX: Baxter Press, 2003.

"James Hudson Taylor." Overseas Missionary Fellowship. OMFUSA.com.

John Wesley. *Christianity Today*. www.christianitytoday.com/history/people/denominationalfounder/joh-wesley.html).

Lewis, Phillip V. *Transformational Leadership: A New Model for Total Church Involvement*. Nashville: Broadman & Holman Publishers, 1996.

Loeb, Marshall and Stephen Kindel. *Leadership for Dummies: A Reference for the Rest of Us!* Foster City, CA: IDG Books, 1999.

McNeal, Reggie. *A Work of Heart: Understanding How God Shapes Spiritual Leaders*. San Francisco: Jossey-Bass Publishers, 2000.

Quilkin, Robertson. *Life in the Spirit*. Nashville: Broadman & Holman Publishers, 2000.

Macchia, S. A. *Becoming a Healthy Church: Ten Traits of a Vital Ministry*. Grand Rapids, MI: Baker Publishing Group, 2003.

Marty, Martin E. *Christianity Today*. Christianitytoday.com/history/theologians/martin-luther.html.

Maxwell, John C. *Developing the Leaders around You: How to Help Others Reach Their Full Potential*. Nashville: Thomas Nelson Publishers, 1995.

Maxwell, John C. *Developing the Leader Within You*. Nashville: Thomas Nelson Publishers, 1993.

McCarty, Doran C., and George W. Knight. *The Practice of Ministry: A Sourcebook*. Nashville: Seminary Extension of the Southern Baptist Seminaries, 1995.

Meyer, F. B. *New Testament Commentary: 1 Corinthians*. Baker Books, 1979.

Miller, Calvin. *The Empowered Leader: 10 Keys to Servant Leadership*. Nashville: Broadman & Holman Publishers, 1995.

Miller, Herb. *Leadership Is the Key: Unlocking Your Effectiveness in Ministry*. Nashville: Abingdon Press, 1997.

_____. *Ministers as Leaders*. Nashville TN: Broadman Press, 1984. (Explores leadership styles based on biblical foundations, leadership practices, follower styles, and congregational teams.)

_____. *Mission-Centered Leadership: Translating Vision into Reality*. Nashville TN: Moench Center for Church Leadership, 2000. (SkillTrack® Leadership)

Moffat, James. *New Testament Commentary Series*. 1938.

Montana, Patrick J., and Bruce H. Charnov. *Management* (Business Review Series). Hauppauge, NY: Barron's, 2000.

Morrison, Emily Kittle. *Leadership Skills: Developing Volunteers for Organizational Success*. Tucson, AZ: Fisher Books, 1994.

Munger, Robert Boyd. *Leading from the Heart: Lifetime Reflections on Spiritual Development*. Downers Grove, IL: InterVarsity Press, 1995.

"No Reserves. No Retreats. No Regrets." *Daily Bread*, December 31, 1988; *The Yale Standard*, Fall 1970 edition.

Nour, D., and Freeway Guides. *Effective Networking: Turn Relationships into Results!* Los Angeles: Freeway Guides, 2008.

Perkins, Dennis N. T. *Leading at the Edge: Leadership Lessons from the Extraordinary Saga of Shackleton's Antarctic Expedition*. New York: AMACOM, 2000.

Phillips, Donald T. *Lincoln on Leadership: Executive Strategies for Tough Times*. New York: Warner Books, 1991.

Plummer, Robert L. *New Testament Greek Words*. B & H Publishing. 1914.

Powell. Paul W. *Getting the Lead Out of Leadership: Principles of Leadership for the Church Today*. Tyler, TX: Paul W. Powell, 1997.

Reiland, Dan. *Spiritual Gifts: A Tool to Discover Your Place in Ministry*. Atlanta: Injoy, Inc., 1998.

Reese, Ed. "James Hudson Taylor." Wholesomewords.org/missions/biotaylor2.html.

Richardson, Ronald W. *Creating a Healthier Church*. Minneapolis: Fortress Press, 1996.

Robertson, A. T. *New Testament Word Pictures*. Zondervan. 1982.

Roxburgh, A. J., F. Romanuk, and Leadership Network (Dallas). *The Missional Leader: Equipping Your Church to Reach a Changing World*. San Francisco: Jossey-Bass Publishers, 2006.

Schaller, Lyle E. *Getting Things Done: Concepts and Skills for Leaders*. Nashville: Abington, 1986.

Scholtes, Peter R. *The Leader's Handbook: A Guide to Inspiring Your People and Managing Daily Workflow*. New York: McGraw-Hill Companies, Inc., 1998.

Senge, Peter M., and George Roth. *The Dance of Change: The Challenges to Sustaining Momentum in Learning Organizations*. New York: Bantam Doubleday Dell Publishing Group, 1999.

Senge, Peter M. *The Fifth Discipline: The Art & Practice of the Learning Organization*. New York, Currency Doubleday, 1994.

Senge, Peter M. *The Fifth Discipline Fieldbook: Strategies and Tools for Building a Learning Organization*. New York: Bantam Doubleday Dell Publishing Group, 1994.

Shawchuck, Norman, and Roger Heuser. *Managing the Congregation: Building Effective Systems to Serve People*. Nashville: Abingdon Press, 1996.

Spencer-Jones, H. D. *1 Corinthians*. London; New York: Funk & Wagnalls Company. 1909.

Spears, Larry C., ed. *Reflections on Leadership: How Greenleaf's Theory of Servant Leadership Influenced Today's Top Management Thinkers*. New York: John Wiley and Sons, Inc., 1995.

Spears, Larry C., and Michele Lawrence, eds. *Focus on Leadership: Servant Leadership for the 21st Century*. New York: John Wiley & Sons, Inc., 2002.

Stacker, Joe R., and Bruce Grubbs. *Pastoral Leadership Skills for Growing Churches*. Nashville: Convention Press, 1988.

Stazesky, Richard C. "George Washington, Genius in Leadership," *The Washington Papers*. February 22, 2000. www.gwpapers.virginia.edu.

Sweet, Leonard. *I Am a Follower: The Way, Truth, and Life of Following Jesus*. Nashville: Thomas Nelson. 2012.

Swindoll, Chuck. *Leadership: Influences That Inspire*. Waco, TX: Word Books, 1985.

Stagich, Timothy. *Transformative Leadership and High-Synergy Motivation*. Chula Vista, CA: Aventine Press, 2003.

Swain, Bernard. *Liberating Leadership: Practical Styles for Pastoral Ministry*. San Francisco: Harper & Row Publishers, 1986.

Tokunaga, Paul. *Invitation to Lead: Guidelines for Emerging Asian American Leaders*. Downers Grove, IL: InterVarsity Press, 2003.

Towns, Elmer. "Casting Vision & Mobilizing Leaders." Global Church Learning Center (www.GCLC.tv), 2015.

Turner, William B. *The Learning of Love: A Journey toward Servant Leadership*. Macon, GA: Smith & Helwys, 2000.

Wagner, C. Peter. *Your Spiritual Gifts Can Help Your Church Grow*. Ventura, CA: Gospel Light, 1995.

Warren, Rick. The Purpose-Driven Church: Growth without Compromising Your Message and Mission. Grand Rapids, MI: Zondervan Publishing House, 1995.

Webb, Henry. Deacons: Servant Models in the Church, updated edition. Nashville: Broadman & Holman Publishers, 2001.

White, Ernest O. Becoming a Christian Leader. Nashville: Convention Press, 1985.

Williams, James D., with Lloyd Elder. Coaching Leadership: Building a Winning Ministry Team. Nashville: Moench Center for Church Leadership, 1999.

Wilkes, C. Gene. Jesus on Leadership: Becoming a Servant Leader. Nashville: LifeWay Press, 1996.

Woods, C. Jeff. Better Than Success: 8 Principles of Faithful Leadership. Valley Forge PA: Judson Press, 2001.

More Dynamic Books By
Kenneth C. Ulmer

Training to Win: A Spiritual Guide to Victorious Living

The Champion in You

The Anatomy of God

SOAP Journal

Inspired By Tozer

In His Image

The Power of Money

Knowing God's Voice

Passionate God

CD/DVD Series

Fasting: Series
Prayer and Fasting: Series
Captivated (CD)
The Kingdom of God: Series
Lordship: The Series
The Pain and Power of Praise: The Series
Old School Love In A Hip Hop World: The Series
Be Happy Series: Happy Is Here
Driven By A Dream: The Series

**Books Can Be Found On
Amazon or shop at www.faithfulcentral.com**

More Dynamic Books By
Dr. James O. Davis

We Are the Church: The Untold Story of God's Global Awakening
(with Dr. Leonard Sweet)

*How to Make Your Net Work: Tying Relational Knots
for Global Impact*

Scaling Your Everest: Lessons from Sir Edmund Hillary

*Gutenberg to Google: The Twenty Indispensable Laws of
Communication*

What to Do When the Lights Go Out

Signposts on the Road to Armageddon

It's a Miraculous Life!

12 Big Ideas

Living Like Jesus

The Pastor's Best Friend: The New Testament Evangelist

The Preacher's Summit

Pathway To Personal Power With God

Beyond All Limits: The Synergistic Church for a Planet in Crisis
(with Dr. Bill Bright)

Great Commission Study Bible
(with Dr. Ben Lerner)

**All Books Are Found On
Amazon and on www.JamesODavis.com**

An Ancient Truth Revealed to a Modern Generation!

This message is not about ceremony. It's not about ritual. It's about unwrapping the gifts, the blessings your heavenly Father has stored up for you! In *The Forgotten Baptism*, you will discover:

- His path for your personal progress!
- His provision for your professional success!
- His plan for your public victory!

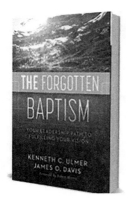

IF YOU'RE A FAN OF THIS BOOK, WILL YOU HELP ME SPREAD THE WORD?

There are several ways you can help me get the word out about the message of this book...

■ Post a 5-Star review on Amazon, Goodreads and other places that come to mind.

■ Write about the book on your Facebook, Twitter, Instagram, Google+, any social media sites you regularly use.

- If you blog, consider referencing the book, or publishing an excerpt from the book with a link back to my website. https://www.faithfulcentral.com

- Recommend the book to friends – word of mouth is still the more effective form of advertising.

- When you're in a bookstore, ask them if they carry the book. The book is available through all major distributors, so any bookstore that does not have it in stock can easily order it.

- Purchase additional copies to give away as gifts.